Lateranense

lla Tavola Sesta col numero 4.

Front Endleaves: Actual Size Detail, *Catalogue Number* 7.

TAVOLA SETTIMA (Drawing 7).

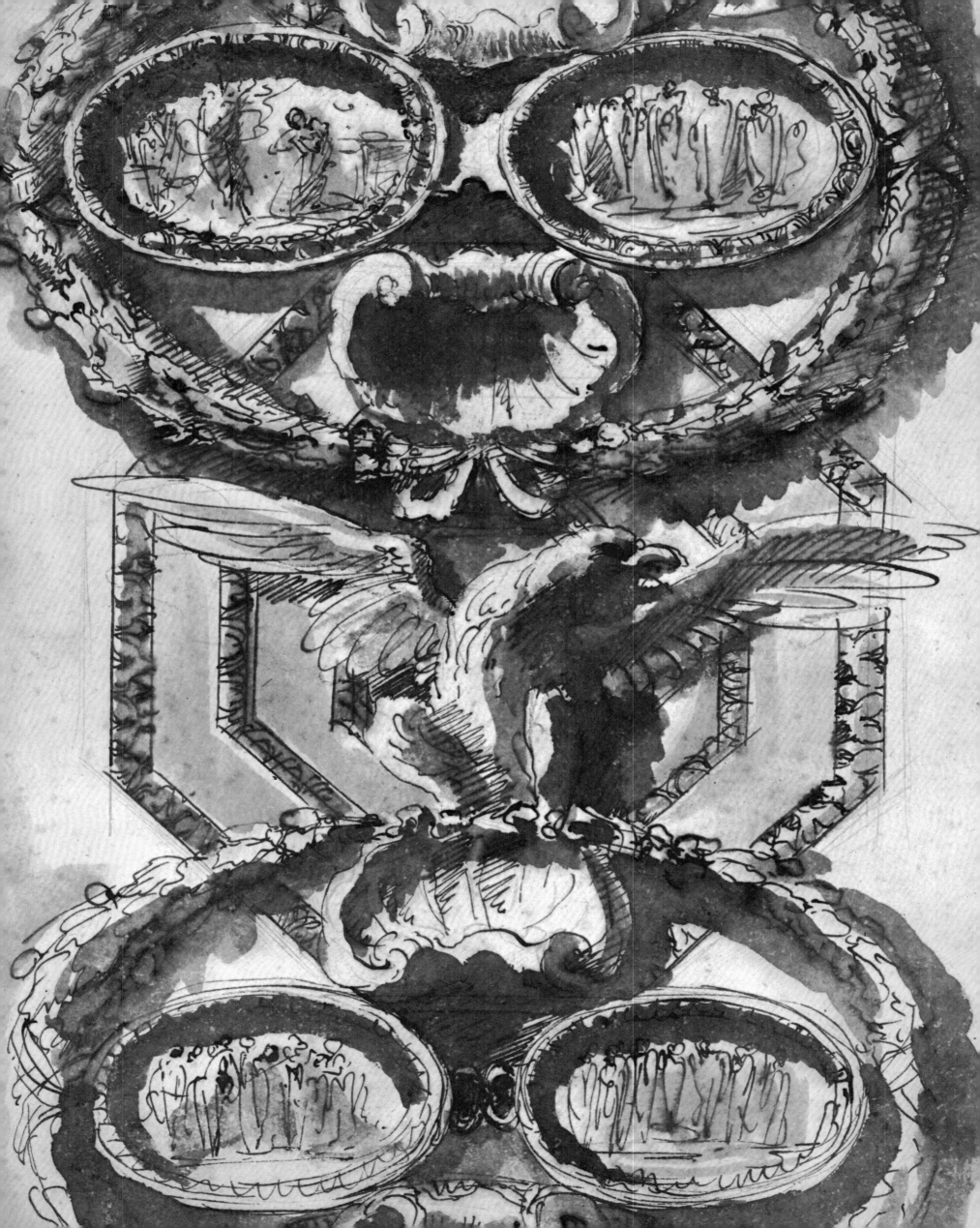

the Arthur M. Sackler Collection

PIRANESI

Drawings and Etchings
at the Avery Architectural Library
Columbia University, New York

A Circulating Exhibition: October, 1975-December, 1978

This Exhibition and Catalogue have been made possible through the cooperation of the Avery Architectural Library, New York, The International Exhibitions Foundation, Washington, D. C., and the Arthur M. Sackler Foundation, New York.

Edited by: Lois Katz and Jessica Berman
Designed by: Sandra Stern

Library of Congress Catalog Card Number: 75-27736

Composition by Southern New England Typographic Service, Incorporated

Printing by The Meriden Gravure Company

Frontispiece: Actual Size Detail, *Catalogue Number 18.*

TAVOLA DECIMANOVA (Drawing 19).

The Avery Architectural Library
and the
Arthur M. Sackler Foundation
dedicate this catalogue to
the memory of
RUDOLF WITTKOWER (1901-1971)

Contents

Piranesi's genius will long be celebrated. His was an epochal achievement, a unique vision of what was to come. For centuries he opened men's minds to the vistas that his imagination explored and that his hand recorded. He brilliantly wedded acid to copper and ink to paper in a bold but frightening statement on man's fate.

Carceri was more prophecy than phantasy. Historically, the Chinese painter had viewed man not in a literal but rather in a philosophical sense, and portrayed him proportioned to the overwhelming grandeur of nature. Piranesi, in his day, redressed the proportions of Western man in a prophetic anticipation of modern man's spiritual as well as physical imprisonment in the steel and stone, in the grinding stresses of the Industrial Revolution that was to to come.

As all great artists, Piranesi linked an appreciation of the past, his *Antichità romane*, with his love of his present, the *Vedute di Roma*, and these were linked to his *Carceri*, which projected his vision into the future. *Carceri* freed Piranesi from the constraints of literal architecture and in its vast perspectives mourns the constraints of body and spirit which were soon to be visited upon that glorious dream — the individual, the Renaissance man.

Appreciation of Piranesi's genius grows both with time and with exposure to its manifestations. This collection of his work has afforded us a unique opportunity to have and to hold the beautiful fruits of a creative imagination. This was then crowned by a unique privilege of experiencing the rediscovery and acquisition of twenty-three of twenty-five heretofore un-known original Piranesi wash drawings. These were his plans for submission to Pope Clement XIII for the expansion of Rome's ancient Basilica of S. Giovanni in Laterano, one of the oldest and most important churches in Christendom. Professor Rudolf Wittkower considered these rare drawings "one of the greatest Piranesi discoveries in many, many years."

One must be grateful for the turn of history which thus enabled us to bring together the bulk of Piranesi's oeuvre. It is also most fitting that it shall henceforth be preserved and studied in that great repository of art historical and architectural literature — the Avery Library of Columbia University. For the pleasures that these privileges have brought us we have many to thank. We want to particularly express our appreciation and gratitude to two men whose talents, penetrating knowledge and devoted efforts made all this possible: Adolf K. Placzek, head of the Avery Library at Columbia, and Herbert Mitchell, Bibliographer of the Avery Library.

Our Piranesi exhibition was dedicated to Rudolf Wittkower, acknowledged by all for his scholarship and leadership, and, by those fortunate enough to know him, for his encompassing gracious humanity. A dedication to this learned man is in effect a consecration of these works of art to those who, hopefully, all of us serve — the students and scholars of today and tomorrow.

Arthur M. Sackler, M.D.

May, 1975

The Introduction

Piranesi and his "opere varie:" Drawings and Etchings

Among the stellar names of the eighteenth century, the name of Giovanni Battista Piranesi (1720–1778) shines with particular brightness into our day and our sensibility. It is above all his awesome visions of fantastic prisons — his *Carceri d' invenzione* — which have become part of the twentieth century imagination. In Vincent Scully's words, they represent "the end of the old, humanist, man-centered world with its fixed values — and the beginning of the mass age of modern history, with its huge environments and rushing continuities." But it is not only for his *Carceri* that he is remembered. They are only part of a vast *oeuvre*. His grandiose views of ancient and Baroque Rome represent a pictorial world of power and contrast, subtlety and drama rare in the history of art. Classicism, Baroque, Rococo, Romanticism, and indeed, the modern vision seem to fuse into one style. No wonder then, that we find ourselves in the midst of what can be called a veritable Piranesi revival. The series of fine Piranesi exhibitions and the public response to them are the best evidence. There were, in quick succession, the exhibition mounted by Smith College in Northampton, Mass. (1961), followed by exhibitions in Turin (1961–1962), the Bibliothèque Nationale in Paris (1962), Bologna (1963), Rome (1967–1968), the British Museum (1968), Princeton University (1971) and finally Columbia University's exhibition of March–April 1972 from which this catalogue derives.

Giovanni Battista Piranesi was born near Mestre on the Italian mainland opposite Venice in 1720. He was definitely a Venetian in spirit — like Giorgione, like Titian, like Tintoretto and above all, like his somewhat older contemporary, Giovanni Battista Tiepolo (1696-1770), in whose atelier he is said to have worked for a short time. We know little about his early years. He went to Rome in 1740 where he soon began the study of ancient Roman architecture. It is to the antiquities of Rome, not of Greece, that his partisanship, his enthusiasm and his love belonged. His early expectations of becoming a successful architect were disappointed. He turned his full passion to drawing and etching. At twenty-three, in 1743, he published his first effort, the *Prima parte di architetture e prospettive*. It did not prove a success. Penniless, he had to go back to Venice.

In 1745 Piranesi managed to return to the center of his world, Rome, where he spent the rest of his life. It was some time during this period that he conceived and executed the fourteen etchings of his *Carceri*, the famous masterpieces of colossal spaces, overwhelming volume, complex perspective and unspoken horror and defiance. He later — around 1760 — reworked the plates, adding not only significant details such as torture instruments, but also deepening the shadows and making compositional re-arrangements. These changes of mood, composition and even technique are of course of the highest interest, particularly when seen juxtaposed as we shall on the following pages. Piranesi also produced two more plates, bringing the number to sixteen. It should also be reiterated that these changes, roughly eighteen years later, were made onto the original copper plates and that therefore no more prints of the first state could be produced. These prints of the first state of the *Carceri* became thus quite rare.

Piranesi next started on several publications, among them the four-volume work of the *Antichità romane*, but above all on the great series of Roman views, the *Vedute di Roma*, on which he was to work his entire life. There were finally one hundred thirty-five views in all, an inexhaustible font of archaeological knowledge and of pure aesthetic delight. Noteworthy also is the ever increasing technical mastery through thirty years of consistent effort. There is, in these prints, also a gradual darkening, descending towards a tragic world view. The progress of this work is recorded in his periodically published *Cataloghi* — really advertisements for his available prints — of which the one shown in this volume as part of the Sackler Collection records sixty-three plates. Piranesi was an amazingly productive artist. According to Hyatt Mayor, he created no less than nine hundred ninety-one copper plates. When he died in 1778, he was at the height of his fame. His son Francesco (1758–1810) carried on his work. He and his younger brother Pietro not only completed some of their father's unfinished projects, but also continuously re-issued the older works from the plates in their possession. Much of this was done from Paris where they had moved their print shop and the plates in 1799. There the plates remained until 1839 when they were returned to Rome where sets were continuously printed until the twentieth century. Eventually Europe seemed flooded with Piranesi prints (this of course is no longer the case) but in Hyatt Mayor's words, "the nineteenth century tired of seeing his great, emphatic etchings everywhere; today, however, his volcanic obsessions are no longer consulted as records of fact but are cherished for the grandeur of their intensely personal vision."

Piranesi was also a trained architect, quite in the tradition of Italian art whose supreme masters from Giotto through Raphael and Leonardo to Michelangelo so often combine several skills, among them those of practical architecture. As an architect, however, Piranesi could not reach the mastery nor the success of his etchings. Circumstances combined against him. Rome, in the second half of the eighteenth century, was no longer a center of large-scale architectural activity. Piranesi's growing fame as a graphic artist may have worked against him rather than for him as far as architectural commissions were concerned. Proud, hot-headed and stubborn, he was also hardly the person to encourage overbearing clients. His only major work is the basically rather austere and dry rebuilding of Santa Maria del Priorato on the Aventine Hill (1764–1767); the manuscript account book for the project is in the Avery Library. This was done at the order of Cardinal Giovanni Battista Rezzonico, fellow Venetian and the nephew of the then Pope, Clement XIII.

Piranesi's only other major architectural project was never executed but both some sketches and the presentation drawings for it survived. These sketches have been, for some time, at the Morgan Library in New York. The presentation drawings are the *pieces de resistance* of the Sackler Collection in the Avery Library. They are the drawings shown and described on the following pages. The project to which they relate is the expansion of the choir of S. Giovanni in Laterano, one of Western Christendom's oldest and most prestigious churches, one of the five patriarchal churches of Rome. Since its founding by the Emperor Constantine it had had an incredible history of destructions, rebuildings, fires, restorations and alterations. The present form of the nave is largely the work of one of the major masters of the Roman Baroque, Francesco Borromini (1599–1667). It was, however, long felt that the medieval apse of the great edifice was inadequate for its vast ceremonial requirements. It was to this need that Piranesi — on Clement XIII's instruction in 1764 — addressed himself. The grandiose project of a new choir and sanctuary was never realized. Clement XIII died in 1769 and with the passing from power of the Rezzonico family Piranesi's architectural patronage was over. The choir of S. Giovanni in Laterano remained too small until the late nineteenth century, when it was finally thoroughly rebuilt under Leo XIII and consecrated in 1885.

The presentation drawings for Piranesi's project had in the meantime disappeared. Nothing is known of their fate for nearly two centuries, nor do they bear any collectors' marks or stamps. They were twenty-five in all, submitted to the pope's nephew, the aforementioned Cardinal Giovanni Battista Rezzonico, but two (which would have borne the numbers 13 and 24) are missing. They are not all entirely by Piranesi's hand; in some places it is apparent that the conscientious but dry hand of pupils filled in the details for the impatient master. No less than six variants for the choir and sanctuary area are suggested in the plans. Four drawings are proposals for a grand papal altar and baldacchino, in the tradition of Gianlorenzo Bernini's baldacchino for St. Peter's. Piranesi's deep attachment to the Roman Baroque is evident; not only from the style and detailing of the drawings themselves, but also from the scrupulous respect shown in the project to Borromini's existing nave. This is clearly evident in the longitudinal section (*Catalogue Number 5*) which carries Borromini's entablature and fluted Corinthian pilasters into the expanded choir (*Catalogue Numbers 8 and 15*). There is in Piranesi also the powerfully emerging Neo-Classic spirit, looking forward to the end of the eighteenth century and back to Andrea Palladio. This is particularly apparent in some of the hard, almost harsh design elements of the projects. The unusual colonnade separating the ambulatory from the sanctuary (*Catalogue Numbers 10 and 23*) is a Neo-Classic feature. There is, of course, in these drawings also the infinite charm of Piranesi's Venetian heritage, the Tiepolo-like delicacy and playfulness of the decorative frames, the illusionism of its seemingly curling paper on the borders (*Catalogue Numbers 9, 10 and 14*), the Rococo spirit of the vignettes which contain the captions and the scale.

The descriptions in the catalogue are by Professor Dorothea Nyberg of Barnard College. Measurements have been taken to the borders ruled by brown ink. Inscriptions are given in the original orthography. The drawings themselves were in rather poor condition when they were acquired by the Avery Library, but were expertly restored through Dr. Sackler's generosity. Professor Nyberg's descriptions, however, refer to the physical condition in which they were received.

All of the drawings and etchings recorded in this catalogue are part of the Arthur M. Sackler collection at the Avery Library, Columbia University's great library of architecture and the decorative arts. Founded and endowed in 1890 by Samuel Putnam Avery, it had always been particularly rich in Piranesi holdings. In 1970, the Avery Library became the beneficiary of the first great gift from Dr. and Mrs. Sackler. It consisted of the collection of most of Piranesi's major works in their early states up to 1764, as dated and described by Mr. Herbert Mitchell in the catalogue at the end of this volume. Added to this was the rare set of first state *Carceri*. In 1971, Dr. and Mrs. Sackler surpassed even this splendid gift and donated the twenty-three architectural drawings which had become available. The very existence of these drawings had been known only for a few years. Support of the most generous sort was required if they were to come to the great center of Piranesi treasures, New York City, and to be placed into the unique research facilities of the Avery Library. Dr. Sackler provided this support. The first public showing of these singularly important drawings took place at Columbia on March 21, 1972.

Dr. and Mrs. Sackler's donations to Columbia were made in honor of Professor Rudolf Wittkower who, as Chairman from 1956 to 1969, had done so much to develop a great Department of Art History and Archaeology at Columbia University and who had devoted so much of his energy and wisdom to bring into being a new generation of American art historians. Rudolf Wittkower had always had a pronounced interest in Piranesi. In fact, his essay "Piranesi as Architect" for the Smith College exhibition catalogue took a fresh look at Piranesi as a practicing builder. Furthermore, it dealt thoroughly with the already mentioned account book for Santa Maria del Priorato in the Avery collection. When the first Sackler gift arrived, Professor Wittkower was delighted. It was given to honor him in life — not only as a scholar and as a teacher, but also as a great human being of rare charm, power and compassion. The first state *Carceri* and the drawings have now become a memorial to him: Rudolf Wittkower died suddenly on October 11, 1971 — the very day on which he gave his seal of enthusiastic approval to the drawings he had just seen for the first time. The exhibition and its catalogue have now been dedicated to his memory. It is a small token of gratitude when compared with our debt to him — but a deeply felt one.

Thanks must go to Dorothea Nyberg who, as chairman of the Piranesi exhibition committee of 1972 was responsible for the initial catalogue; to Jane Sabersky, curator of Columbia's art properties who organized the original exhibition; to Alexander Stoia, formerly Assistant Vice President of Columbia University; to Barry Byers, formerly of the Metropolitan Museum of Art, who restored the drawings; and last but not least to Herbert Mitchell, Bibliographer of Avery Library, whose scholarship on Piranesi has been of immense help, not only in all activities of the Avery Library, but in the preparation of this catalogue as well.

The introduction to several of the entries written for the 1972 catalogue have been retained and bear their authors' signatures: Martin Filler, John E. Mortensen and Charlotte Rice. All other compilations and notes are by Mr. Mitchell.

Adolf K. Placzek
Avery Librarian

May, 1975

A Note about the Etchings

In 1970, Dr. Arthur M. Sackler presented a splendid early set* of Piranesi's works to the Avery Library. Sets like this, printed midway in Piranesi's career and containing everything he had thus far published, are extremely rare. These eight unnumbered volumes, but numbered here for convenience of identification, and arranged roughly by date of publication, comprise: Volume[I]** *Opere varie* with four separate works in one volume: *Prima parte, Carceri d'invenzione, Trofei di Ottaviano Augusto, Antichità romane de tempi della Republica;* Volume [II] *Vedute di Roma;* Volumes [III-VI] *Antichità romane* with its numbered Volumes I-IV, Volume [VII] with three parts bound in one volume: *Lapides Capitolini, Rovine del castello dell' Acqua Giulia* and *Emissario del Lago Albano;* and, Volume [VIII], also with three parts bound in one volume: *Antichità d' Albano* (title only), *Di due spelonche* and *Antichità di Cora.* All are bound in the original publishers' marbled boards and lightly sewn.

Before attempting to determine the year this set was made up and sold, some problems of dating in Piranesi's publications — a complex, fascinating and often baffling subject — must be considered. For example, some volumes have no publication dates at all. Moreover, all of Piranesi's etched plates were being constantly reprinted, usually with little or no change on the plate. Therefore, dated and etched title pages retain their original dates over the years. There are few well-defined editions. The actual date of printing of individual etchings or series of etchings is unknown. Furthermore, dates on letterpress titles or other pages can be misleading too. Piranesi, at the time of first publication of a volume, apparently would print vast quantities of the letterpress leaves, enough to last for decades. The etched plates, however, would seem to have been printed from time to time in far smaller quantities, more or less as needed. Plates and printed matter would then be made up into a volume for sale. This would explain why it is that different copies of a work whose letterpress pages are identical may contain etched plates whose appearance varies markedly. These copies may differ in state, type of paper, method of inking or color of ink and such differences should indicate widely separated dates of printing. For instance, in the Sackler set, Volume I of the *Antichità romane* has the standard letterpress leaves. The title page is dated 1756. Page [4] contains the famous list of works available in 1756 (see *Catalogue Number 32*). However, a copy of the etched *Catalogo* which must date from the 1760's appears bound at the end of Volume IV. Also, in this volume, Plates VI–X have been newly numbered. In earlier copies, the latter had appeared as Plates IX–X, VII, VI, VIII respectively. This new numbering, whose date is unknown, was used in all subsequent printings. Finally, a variant of the problem just discussed should be treated separately. On the *Opere varie* title page (letterpress), Piranesi chose to retain the original date (1750) in later editions. Hind distinguished three editions in all (Hind, p. 78–79). The title of the Sackler *Opere varie* corresponds to Hind's third edition (called "Later edition B"). It is perversely dated 1750 although it actually was printed in 1761 or later.

Returning to a consideration of the date of the Sackler set, it is clear that the first seven volumes contain exactly the same works as those listed in the copy of the *Catalogo* (undated as always) bound in Volume IV of the *Antichità romane (Catalogue Number 35)*. Both in the set and in the listing, the *Vedute di Roma* have progressed as far as sixty-three plates. The *Emissario del Lago Albano*, the latest work to be included, is complete with its nine plates and is so listed in the *Catalogo*, but its date of publication is unclear. No date appears on its title page. Its *Approbatio* (permission to print) however, has the date April 1, 1762. Two of his works, nearly contemporary, took about one year between *Approbatio* and publication, i.e., *Della magnificenza*, 1760–61, and the *Lapides Capitolini*, 1761–62. If the same time span holds true for the *Emissario*, the date of publication should be sometime in 1763. It is quite possible, then, that the first seven volumes were ready for sale in 1763 or early 1764.

The three works in Volume [VIII] do not appear in the *Catalogo* mentioned above. What are their dates of publication? The lone title page of the *Antichità d' Albano* is dated 1764. The *Approvazione* of *Di due spelonche* is dated August 30, 1762. It lacks a date of publication but this would probably be rather late in 1763 or even 1764. As to the *Antichità di Cora*, which is entirely undated, there is some external evidence. Hind reports that the catalogue of 1792 dates (*approbatio* ?) 1763 (Hind, p. 85). Arthur Samuel illustrates a copy of the *Catalogo* just like that in the Sackler set but with a fascinating handwritten addition: *Nel mese di Maggio del 1764 si darrano alla luce le Antichità di Cora, e di Albano* (*Piranesi*, second edition, London, 1912, Plate III). This final volume seems to consist of a group of newly published works added to the seven volumes already printed and bound for sale. If all the parts of Volume [VIII] were ready by 1764, it can be safely stated that the whole set could have left Piranesi's shop that year.

There are no bookplates or other evidence of the original ownership. It seems likely however, in view of notations within the volumes, that the set reached Great Britain early on. On Plate LX of Volume II of the *Antichità romane* the following note appears: L. H. 1789 lost Sept. / found Jan.ry 3rd 1790. Further, the title page of Volume I of the *Antichità* is inscribed thus: *Job: Richards / given to A. & F. Richards / Jan. 1808-* (see illustration of *Catalogue Number 32*). The other seven volumes are inscribed: *A.F.R.* (A. & F. Richards?).

The Sackler collection at Avery Library contains one further volume which is not part of the same marbled board volumes referred to above with the notations and inscriptions just described. It was, however, added to the collection in 1973 and is a copy of *Della magnificenza ed architettura de' romani* with supplement.

---

*Two of its volumes, however, namely *Della magnificenza ed architettura de' romani* and *Il Campo Marzio dell' antica Roma*, apparently incomplete, have remained in private hands though their present location is unknown.

**See *Abbreviations and Symbols* for explanation of small brackets appearing in text.

Two lists of the watermarks that occur in the paper used in Piranesi's work are known to me — that in Hind (Hind, p. 34 and Plate I) and in the Colnaghi Piranesi catalogue, 1973/74 (Colnaghi, the final six pages, unnumbered). Those legible in the present volumes are almost wholly of Hind's type 3: fleur-de-lis within a double circle with a monogram "CB" above. Of those partly legible, a double circle at least can be seen. Colnaghi's list gives five versions of Hind's type 3 and gives them as numbers 7, 9, and 10 A-C. In their catalogue these watermarks appear on an early impression of plates from the *Antichità romane* and on other works printed in the 1760's and into the 1770's. This conforms in general to the date of printing assumed for the Sackler volumes. The several exceptions will be listed in the volume descriptions.

Impressions

Andrew Robison has concluded after extensive comparisons that Piranesi preferred different colored inks in the successive periods of his career (Robison I, p. 200–202). He states that from the middle 1750's through the 1760's, Piranesi's inks were dominated by sepia tones. This certainly holds true for the plates under discussion. The ink colors range through browns and sepias with rarely a true black. There is one striking exception. In Volume [VIII], all the etchings except two, a vignette and a plate in *Di due spelonche*, are printed in a rich black.

Herbert Mitchell

May, 1975

The exhibition contains all the drawings and *Carceri*, first and second states, as described in this catalogue, as well as the title pages to each of the sections of the Sackler volumes of etchings also described but not illustrated in the catalogue. Included also in both the exhibition and the catalogue are the sixty-one *Vedute di Roma* which make up part of the Sackler set and have been organized according to the chronology worked out by Mr. Herbert Mitchell.

The Drawings

Catalogue Number 1. TAVOLA P'MA (Drawing 1).

Title Page of Presentation Drawings Embodying Proposals for a New Sanctuary of S. Giovanni in Laterano, Rome

Pianta della Tribuna, del Presbiterio, e dell'Esedra della Basilica Lateranense, immaginati a seconda della gran Nave.

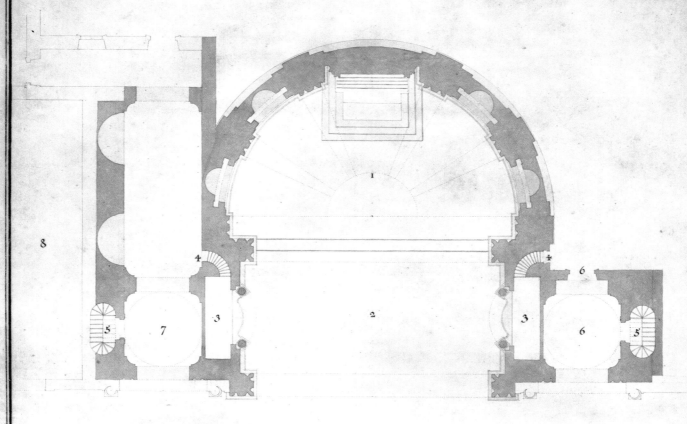

Varj Disegni fatti d'ordine della SANTITÀ DI NOSTRO SIGNORE
PAPA CLEMENTE XIII
nell'anno 1764. dal Cav.re Giovambatista Piranesi Arch.to pe'l compimento
della nuova Basilica Lateranense:
presentati dal medesimo Cav.re nell'anno 1767. a S.E. Monsignor D. Giovambatista Rezzonico
Nipote e Maggiordomo della SANTITÀ SUA

1. Presbiterio elevato due gradi di più dell'Esedra.
2. Esedra al pari della Crociata, di architettura corrispondente a quella della gran Nave.
3. Coro de' Musici di architettura corrispondente a quella de' nicchi de' Apostoli
   che girano intorno alla gran Nave.
4. Scale per salire al coro de' Musici.
5. Scale per salire alle stanze, o conditori delle Reliquie.
6. Atrio, ed ingresso deretano della Basilica.
7. Atrio consimile, che comunica con la Basilica, e con l'andito della Sagrestia.
8. Coro d'inverno de' Canonici.
9. Cappella del Presepio.

Le altre parti si dichiareranno nelle loro respettive elevazioni.

Catalogue Number 2. TAVOLA SEC^DA (Drawing 2).

Cross Section Showing West Wall of Transept and View into Sanctuary

Elevazione ortografica, o sia Fronte della Tribuna e degl'ingressi deretani
della Basilica Lateranense.

I numeri dall'uno fino al dodici circoscrivono l'opera da farsi per gl'ingressi deretani, e per la Tribuna.

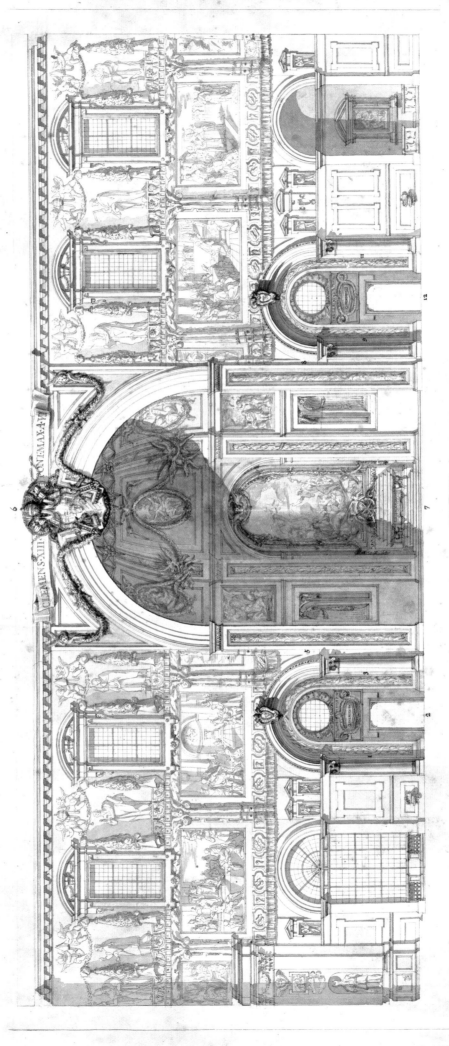

Scala di Palmi Romani CXX.

Cav. G.B. Piranesi fece.

Catalogue Number 3 . TAVOLA TERZA (Drawing 3).

Longitudinal Section Showing South Wall of Sanctuary, with Transept and Beginning of Nave

Tavola Terza

Sezione ortografica di una Tribuna, del Presbiterio, e dell'Eedra, del Presbiterio, e dell'Eedra della Basilica Lateranense *** *** ginati con architettura corrispondente a quella della gran Nave

Cav.^r G.B. Piranesi fece

Catalogue Number 4. TAVOLA QUARTA (Drawing 4).

Plan and View of Sanctuary from the Transept

Pianta della Tribuna, del Presbiterio, e dell'Esedra della Basilica Lateranense
immaginati secondo l'architettura della gran Nave.

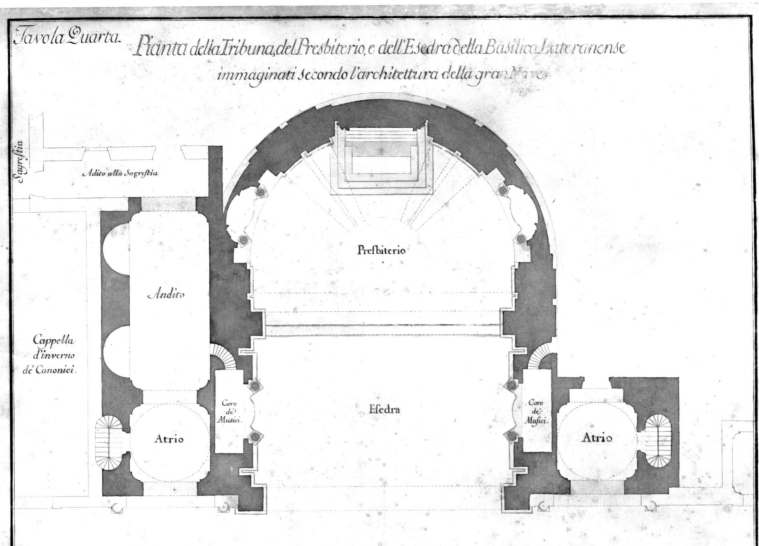

Elevazione ortografica, o sia Fronte della stessa Tribuna
e degli atrj notati nella Pianta.

I numeri dall'uno sino al dodici circoscrivono l'opera da farsi per la Tribuna, e per gli Atrj.

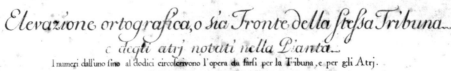

Cav.r G.B. Piranesi fece.

Catalogue Number 5. TAVOLA QUINTA (Drawing 5).

Longitudinal Section Showing South Wall of Sanctuary, with Transept and Beginning of Nave

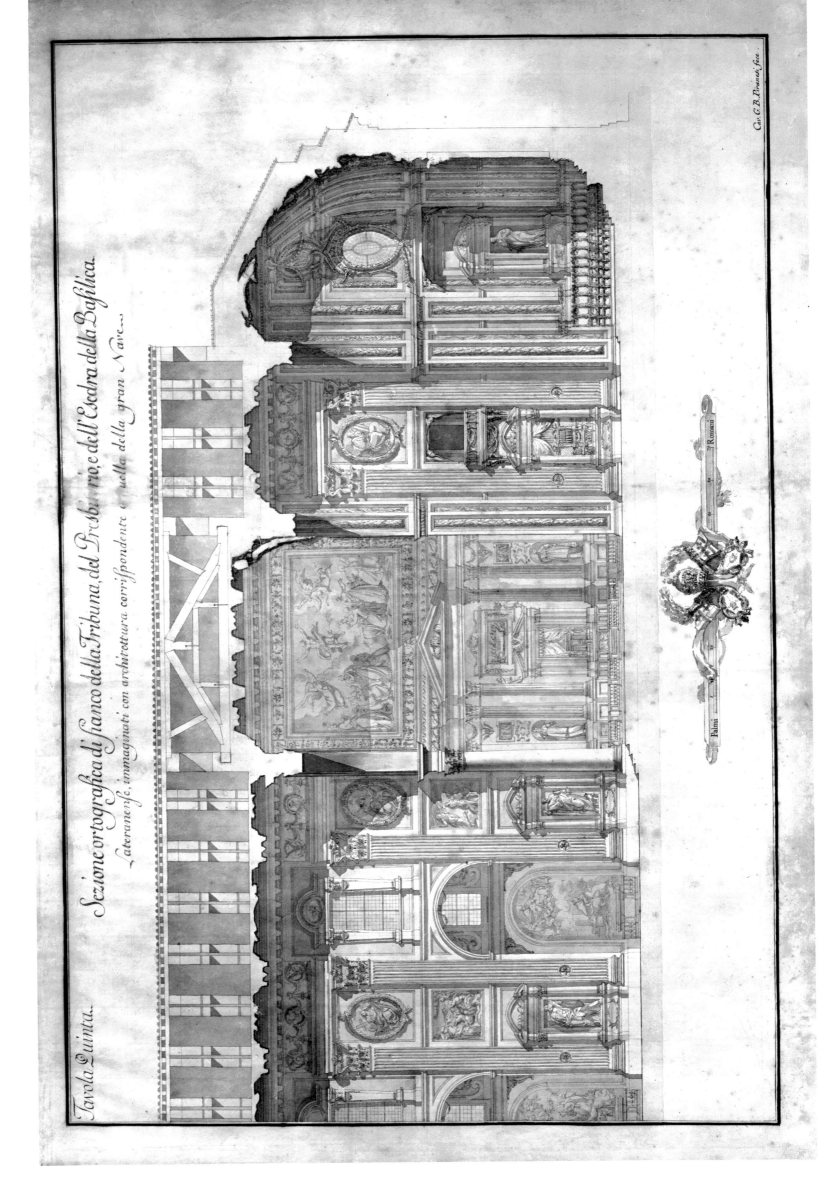

Tavola Quinta.

Sezione ortografica di fianco della Tribuna, del Presbiterio, e dell'Esedra della Basilica.
Lateranense, immaginati con architettura corrispondente a quella della gran Nave.

Palmi

Romani

Cav. G. B. Piranesi fece.

Catalogue Number 6. TAVOLA SESTA (Drawing 6).

Plan of Sanctuary with Screen of Columns and Ambulatory

Tav.
Sesta.

Pianta della Tribuna, del Presbiterio, e dell'Esedra della Basilica Lateranense
immaginati con architettura a seconda di quella della gran Nave.

1. Tribuna.
2. Presbiterio.
3. Esedra architettata, come la gran Nave.
4. Colonnato, e steccato, che separa il Presbiterio dalla Tribuna.
5. Coro de' Musici.
6. Scala per salire al coro de' Musici.
7. Scale per salire ai Conditorj delle Reliquie.
8. Atrj architettati, come le Navi inferiori.
9. Ambulacro fra il Presbiterio, e la Tribuna, archi-
    tettato, come la gran Nave.
10. Porta laterana della Basilica.
11. Porta della Sagrestia.
12. Coro d'inverno de' Canonici.
13. Cappella del Presepio.
14. Ingrandimento di essa, quanto il coro d'inverno.
15. Conditorio della Mensa di Nostro Signor Gesù Cristo.
16. Altar Papale.
17. Recinto, e gradi per difendere al Conditorio delle sacre Teste de' SS. Apostoli Pietro e Paolo.

Cav.r G. B. Piranesi fece.

Catalogue Number 7. TAVOLA SETTIMA (Drawing 7).

Plan and View of Sanctuary from the Transept

Cav.r G.B.Piranesi fece.

Elevazione ortografica di fronte del Presbiterio
della Basilica Lateranense
notato nella sottoposta Pianta, ed accennato nella Tavola Sesta col numero 4.

Pianta della Tribuna, del Presbiterio, è dell'Esedra
della Basilica Lateranense
Le indicazioni delle parti ommesse nella presente Pianta possono vederli nella Tavola VI.

Cav.r G.B.Piranesi fece.

Catalogue Number 8. TAVOLA OTTAVA (Drawing 8).

Longitudinal Section Showing South Wall of Sanctuary, with Transept and Beginning of Nave

Tavola Ottava.

...one ortografica di fianco della Tribuna del ...
e dell'Tribuna della Basilica Lateranense
immaginati con architettura corrispondente a quella della ...

Catalogue Number 9. TAVOLA NONA (Drawing 9).

Cross Section Showing Rear of Apse Facing West

Tavola Nona.

Elevazione della Tribuna della Basilica Lateranense
notata in Pianta nelle Tavole VI. e VII. con le lett. A B C,
ed immaginata con architettura corrispondente
a quella della gran Nave.

1. Porta della Sagrestia. 2. Porta deretana della Basilica. 3. Conditorio della Mensa di Nostro Signor Gesù Cristo.

Palmi .... Romani.

Cav. i. B. Piranesi fece.

Tavola Nona.

Catalogue Number 10. TAVOLA DECIMA (Drawing 10).

Elevation Looking East, Showing the Colonnade Separating the Ambulatory from the Presbytery

Tavola Decima.

Aspetto del di dietro del Recinto del Presbiterio
della Basilica Lateranense
delineato in Pianta nella Tavola VI. e notatovi col numero 4.

Palmi   Romani.

Cav.r G.B. Piranesi fece.

Detail of *Catalogue Number 10*.

TAVOLA DECIMA (Drawing 10).

CLEMENS·XII·PONTIE·MAX
PONTIFICAT·SVI·ANNO·VI

Palmi
10   20   30   40   50   60   70   80   90   100   110   120   130   140
Romani

Cav.r G.B. Piranesi fece.

Catalogue Number 11. TAVOLA UNDECIMA (Drawing 11).

Plan of Sanctuary with Screen of Columns and Ambulatory

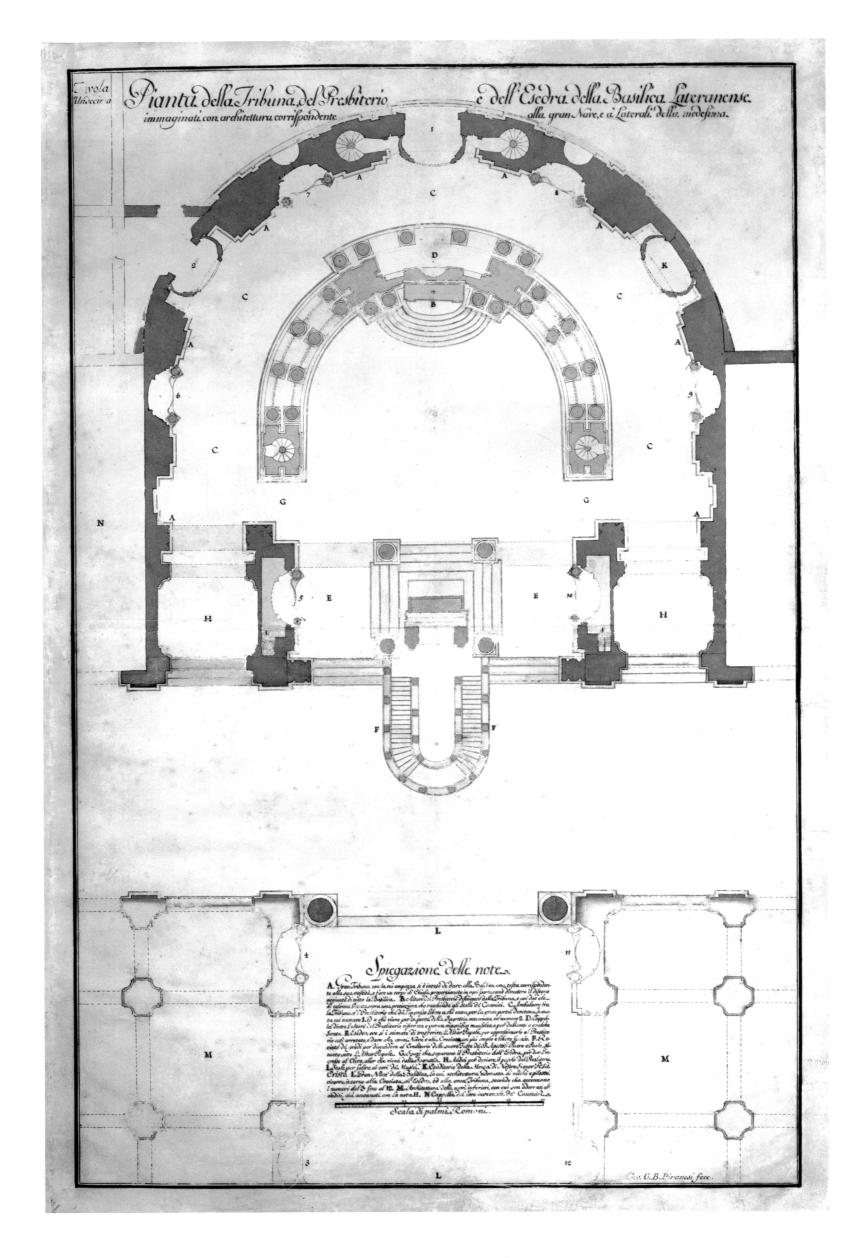

Tavola
Undecima

Pianta della Tribuna, del Presbiterio

immaginati con architettura corrispondente

e dell'Esedra della Basilica Lateranense.

alla gran Nave, e à Laterali della medesima.

Spiegazione delle note.

A. Gran Tribuna, con la cui ampiezza, si è inteso di dare alla Basilica una testa, corrispondente alla sua profila, e fare un corpo di Chiesa, proporzionato in ogni sua parte, come finestra il disegno aggiunto di tutte le Basilica. B. Altare, e Presbiterio disegnati della Tribuna, e con due ale di colonne. Piazza come una, prescrizione che rachiuda gli stalli de' Canonici. C. Ambulacro fra la Tribuna, e 'l Presbiterio che dal luogo più libero a chi entra, per la gran porta, si ertana, annotata col numero 1. D. a chi viene per le porte delle Sagrestia, annotata col numero 2. D. Cappella dietro l'altare del Presbiterio riservata e persona magnifica manifesta, o per dedicarsi e e eredite Sente. E. Esedre, con si è stimate di trasferirvi li Altar Papale, per apprestarsi e 'l Presbiterio così annesso, e dare alla gran Nave e alla Crociata un più ampio e libero spazio. F. Scalinate di gradi per discendere al Confessione delle quatre teste de Ss. Apostoli Pietro e Paolo, situate entro l'Altar Papale. G. Spazi che separano il Presbiterio dell'Esedra, per dar l'ingresso al Chero, allor che viene dalla Sagrestia. H. Anditi per deviare il popolo dal Presbiterio. I. Scale per salire ai cori del Musici. K. Confisteria della Mensa di Nostro Signor Gesu Cristo. L. Gran Nave della Basilica, la cui architettura, ubernata, di nicchi e pilastri ricorre, in tutto la Crociata, all'Esedre, ed alla gran Tribuna, secondo che accennano i numeri dal 3 fino al 12. M. Architettura delle parti inferiori, con cui adoverasi gli anditi, già accennati con la nota H. N. Cappella, del coro invernale de' Canonici.

Scala di palmi Romani.

Cav. G. B. Piranesi fece.

Catalogue Number 12. TAVOLA DUODECIMA (Drawing 12).

Cross Section Showing Projected West Wall of Transept, with Baldacchino Placed Inside Sanctuary Arch

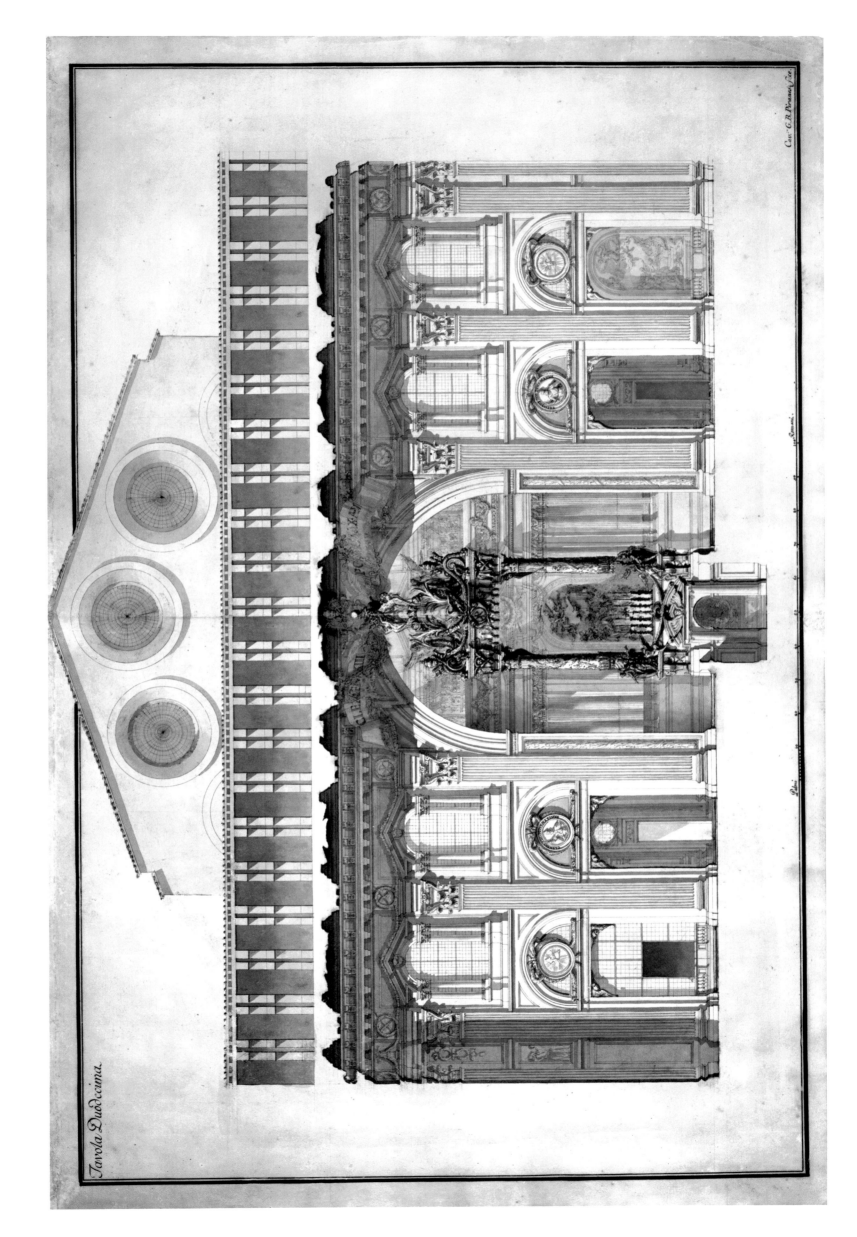

Cav. G. B. Piranesi F.

Palmi

Romani

Detail of *Catalogue Number 12*.

TAVOLA DUODECIMA (Drawing 12).

Catalogue Number 13. TAVOLA DECIMAQUARTA (Drawing 14).*

Plan of Sanctuary with Ambulatory

Pianta della Tribuna, del Presbiterio, e dell'Esedra della Basilica Lateranense, immaginati con architettura corrispondente a quella della gran Nave.

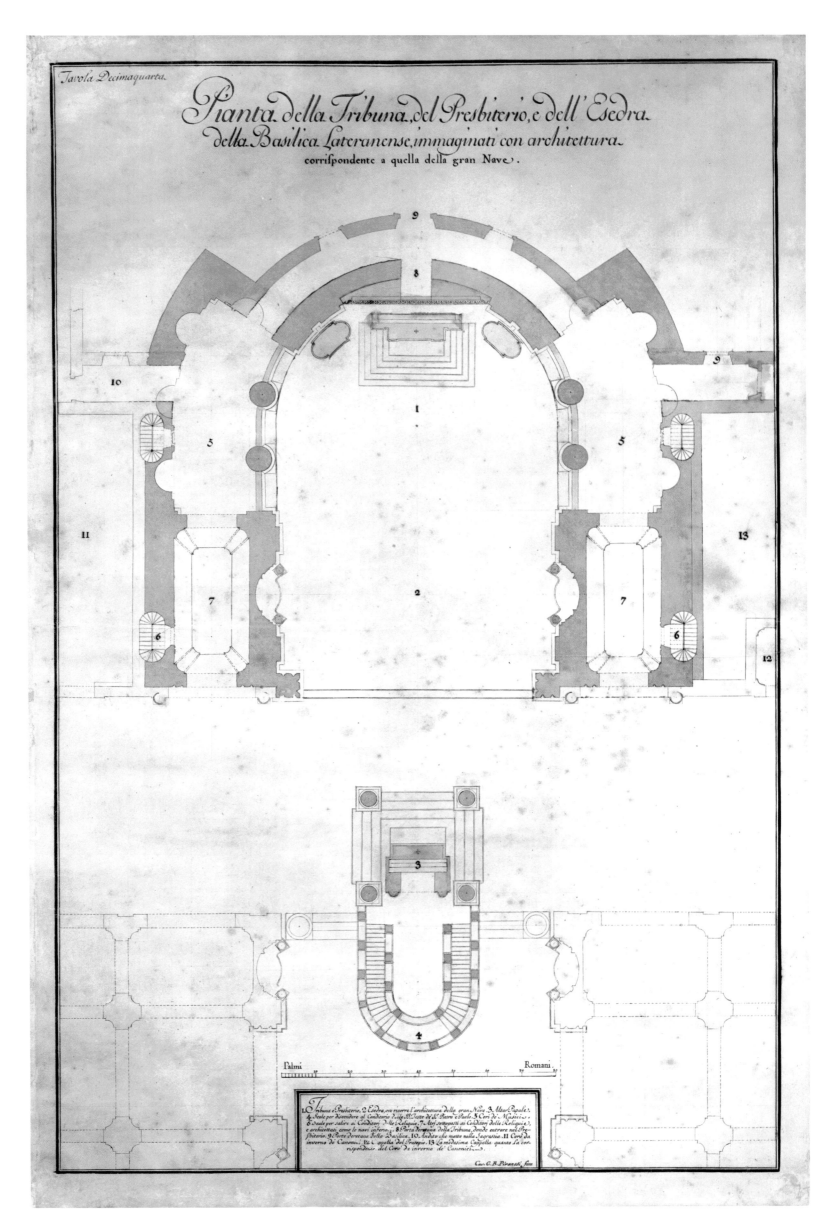

Palmi   Romani.

1. Tribuna e Presbiterio. 2. Esedra, ove ricorre l'architettura della gran Nave. 3. Altar Papale. 4. Scale per discendere al Condotto delle SS. Teste di S. Pietro e Paolo. 5. Cori de' Musici. 6. Scale per salire ai Conditori delle Reliquie. 7. Atrj sotteracci ai Conditori delle Reliquie, e architettati come le navi inferne. 8. Porta Aereana della Tribuna, donde entrare nel Presbiterio. 9. Porte laterani della Basilica. 10. Andito che mette nella Sacristia. 11. Coro da inverno de' Canonici. 12. È quella del Presepio. 13. La medesima Cappella, quanto la corrispondente del Coro da inverno de' Canonici.

Cav. G. B. Piranesi fece

Tavola Decimaquarta.

Catalogue Number 14. TAVOLA DECIMAQUINTA (Drawing 15).

Cross Section Through the Choir, Corresponding to Drawing 14

Elevazione ortografica della Tribuna, e del Presbiterio
della Basilica Lateranense
corrispondente alle Piante, ed alla Sezione, delineate nelle Tavole XII. XIII. XIV.

Cav. G. B. Piranesi f.

Scala di palmi Romani

Detail of *Catalogue Number 14*.

TAVOLA DECIMAQUINTA (Drawing 15).

Catalogue Number 15. TAVOLA DECIMASESTA (Drawing 16).

Longitudinal Section Showing South Wall of Sanctuary, with Transept and Beginning of Nave

Sezione ortographica di franco della Tribuna
del Presbiterio, e dell'Eedra
della Basilica Lateranense
immaginati con architettura corrispondente a quella della gran Nave, e de'lati.

Romani.

1. Vno de'Coretti da mostrar le Sacre Reliquie.
2. Coro De'Musici Della Cappella.

Cav. Gio.B. Piranesi Fece.

Catalogue Number 16. TAVOLA DECIMASETTIMA (Drawing 17).

Plan of Sanctuary

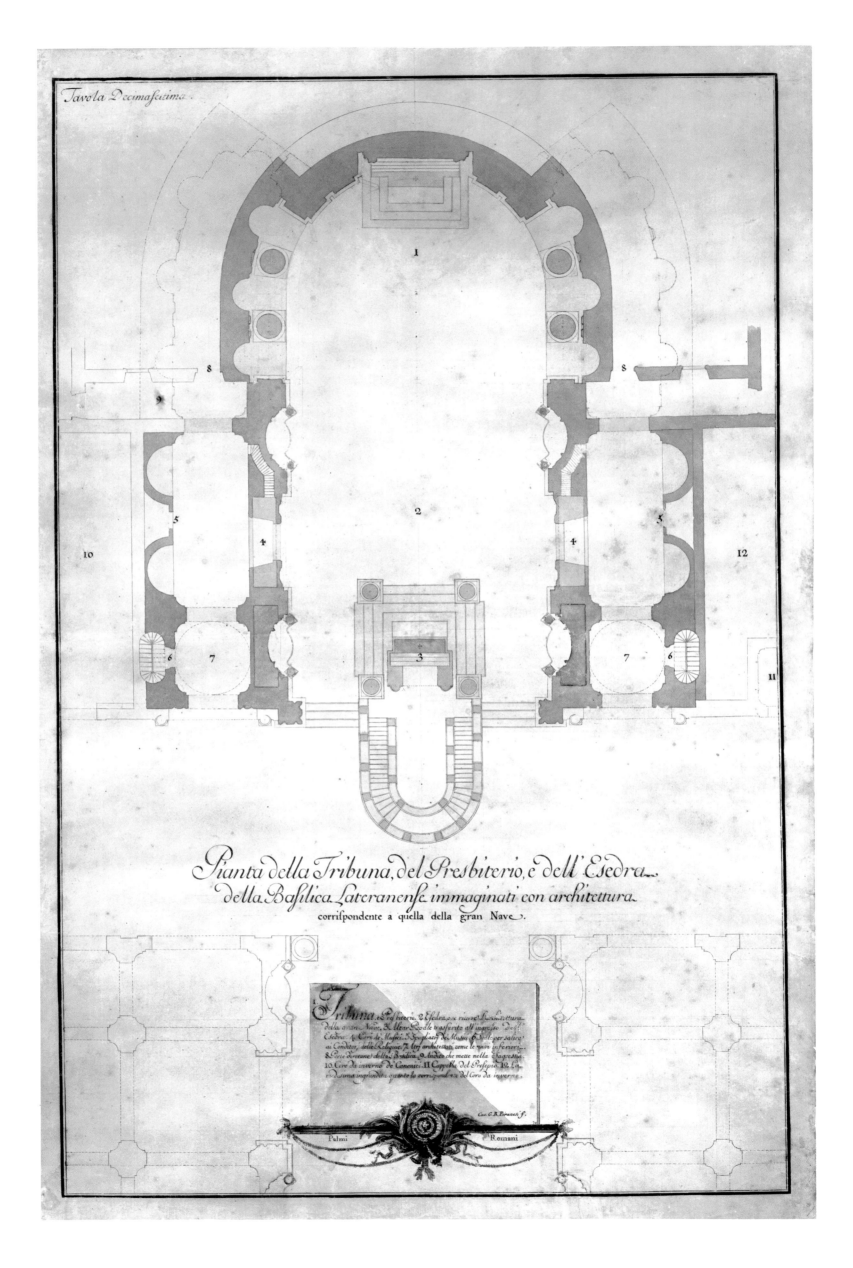

Pianta della Tribuna, del Presbiterio, e dell'Esedra
della Basilica Lateranense immaginati con architettura
corrispondente a quella della gran Nave.

Cav. G.B. Piranesi f.

Palmi   Romani

Catalogue Number 17. TAVOLA DECIMAOTTAVA (Drawing 18).

Longitudinal Section Showing North Wall of Sanctuary, with Transept and Beginning of Nave

Sezione ortografica di fianco della Tribuna, del Presbiterio, e dell'Esedra della Basilica Lateranense, immaginati con architettura corrispondente a quella della gran Nave.

Tavola Decima ottava.

Cav. G.B. Piranesi f.

1. 2. Coretti per mostrar le Sacre Reliquie, che si conservano nella Basilica.
3 Coro de Musici della Cappella.

Catalogue Number 18. TAVOLA DECIMANONA (Drawing 19).

Panel of Vaulting Coffers, Corresponding to Drawing 9

Dimostrazione in grande de' lavori delineati ne' compartimenti della
gran Tribuna che si mostra alla Tavola Nona.

Cav.º G.B. Piranesi fece.

Actual Size Detail, *Catalogue Number 18.*

TAVOLA DECIMANOVA (Drawing 19).

Catalogue Number 19. TAVOLA VIGESIMA (Drawing 20).

Papal Altar and Baldacchino

Altro progetto dell'Altar Papale della Basilica Lateranense
veduto dalla parte della gran nave della stessa Basilica
adornato con un'urna da riporvi le Sacre Teste de' Santi Apostoli Pietro e Paolo.

Cav. G. B. Piranesi fece.

Detail of *Catalogue Number 19*.

TAVOLA VEGESIMA (Drawing 20).

Catalogue Number 20. TAVOLA VIGESIMAPRIMA (Drawing 21).

Plan and Elevation of Papal Altar and Baldacchino

Uno de' progetti dell'Altar Papale, veduto
dalla parte della mensa che riguarda. La

Tribuna, ed inventato sul gusto del Boromino,
secondo il quale è stata rinnovata la Basilica.

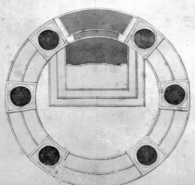

Cav. C. Batta. Piranesi f.

Catalogue Number 21. TAVOLA VIGESIMASECONDA (Drawing 22).

Papal Altar and Baldacchino, Flanked by Elaborate Candelabra

Tavola Vigesimaseconda.

Cav. G. Batta Piranesi fece.

Catalogue Number 22. TAVOLA VIGESIMATERZA (Drawing 23).

Papal Altar and Baldacchino, Flanked by Elaborate Candelabra

Altro progetto dell'Altar Papale della Basilica Lateranense rappresentato e veduto dalla parte della mensa, che riguarda la Tribuna, e inventato su lo Stile del Boromino, secondo il quale è stata rinnovata la Basilica.

Cav. G. Batta Piranesi fece.

Actual Size Detail, *Catalogue Number 22.*

TAVOLA VIGESIMATERZA (Drawing 2 3).

Catalogue Number 23. TAVOLA VIGESIMAQUINTA (Drawing 25).*

Design for Colonnade Separating the Ambulatory from the Presbytery (seen in Drawing 10) with Alternate Version of Attic to Left

*Drawing 24 is missing.

The Etchings

Catalogue Numbers 24a and 25a. THE CARCERI.

Title Plate (Plate 1) States I A and II

Catalogue Number 25b. THE CARCERI.

An Architectural Medley with a Man on the Rack in the Foreground. Plate 2   State I

Presso l'Autore a Strada Felice vicino alla Trinità de' Monti. Fogli Sedici, al prezzo di paoli venti.   Piranesi F.

Catalogue Numbers 24b and 25c. THE CARCERI.

A Vaulted Building with a Staircase Leading Round a Central Column with Barred Window in the Center. Plate 3

States I and II

Catalogue Numbers 24c and 25d. THE CARCERI.

A Lofty Arch with Vista on to an Arcade Surmounted by a Frieze. Plate 4   States I and II

Catalogue Number 25e. THE CARCERI.

A Perspective of Roman Arches with Two Lions Carved in Relief on Stone Slabs on the Foreground. Plate 5   State I

Piranesi F.

Catalogue Numbers 24d and 25f. THE CARCERI.

A Perspective of Arches with a Smoking Fire in the Center. Plate 6   States I and II

Actual Size Detail, *Catalogue Number 25f.*

CARCERI, second state showing the revisions to the first state as seen in *Catalogue Number 24d*.

Catalogue Numbers 24e and 25g. THE CARCERI.

An Immense Interior with Numerous Wooden Galleries and a Drawbridge in the Center. Plate 7   States I and II

Piranesi f.

Catalogue Numbers 24f and 25h. THE CARCERI.

A Vast Interior with Trophies at the Foot of a Broad Staircase and Two Large Flags on the Left. Plate 8   States I and II

Catalogue Numbers 24g and 25i. THE CARCERI.

A Prison Door Surmounted by a Colossal Wheel-shaped Opening, Crossed by Beams. Plate 9   States I and II

Piranesi f.

Catalogue Numbers 24h and 25j. THE CARCERI.

A Vast Gallery with Round Arches and a Group of Prisoners on a Projecting Stone in the Foreground. Plate 10   States I and II

Catalogue Numbers 24i and 25k. THE CARCERI.

A Series of Galleries with Round Arches and a Cranelike Construction of Beams in the Right Foreground. Plate 11   States I and II

Actual Size Detail, *Catalogue Number 25k.*

CARCERI, second state showing the revisions to the first state as seen in *Catalogue Number 24i.*

Catalogue Numbers 24j and 25l. THE CARCERI.

An Arched Chamber with Lower Arches Surmounted by Posts and Chains. Strong Light Entering from the Right. Plate 12   States I and II

Catalogue Numbers 24k and 25m. THE CARCERI.

Colonnaded Interior with a Broad Staircase Divided in Two by a Stone Projection with Barred Window. Plate 13   States I and II

Catalogue Numbers 24l and 25n. THE CARCERI.

A Perspective of Colonnades with Zig-Zag Staircase and Two Figures on Arch Overlooking the Central Flight. Plate 14   States I and II

Catalogue Numbers 24m and 250. THE CARCERI.

Round Arches Springing from a Square Column Ornamented with the Heads of Giants with Rings in their Mouths.

Plate 15   States I and II

Actual Size Detail, *Catalogue Number 250.*

CARCERI, second state showing the revisions to the first state as seen in *Catalogue Number 24m*.

Catalogue Numbers 24n and 25p. THE CARCERI.

A Wide Hall with Low-Timbered Roof in the Foreground from which Hangs a Lantern. Plate 16   States I and II

Catalogue Number 26. CATALOGO

Etched plate containing list of Piranesi's work, State I.

Catalogue Number 32. ANTICHITÀ ROMANE Volume I.

Letterpress title page.

LE ANTICHITÀ
ROMANE
OPERA
DI GIAMBATISTA
PIRANESI
ARCHITETTO VENEZIANO
DIVISA IN QUATTRO TOMI
NEL PRIMO DE' QUALI SI CONTENGONO
GLI AVANZI DEGLI ANTICHI EDIFIZJ DI ROMA
DISPOSTI IN TAVOLA TOPOGRAFICA
SECONDO L'ODIERNA LORO ESISTENZA
ED ILLUSTRATI CO' FRAMMENTI DELL'ANTICA ICNOGRAFIA MARMOREA,
E CON UN INDICE CRITICO DELLA LORO DENOMINAZIONE
ARRICHITO DI TAVOLE SUPPLETORIE
FRALLE QUALI SI DIMOSTRANO

L'elevazione degli steffi avanzi: l'andamento degli antichi Aquedotti nelle vicinanze e nel dentro di Roma, correlativo al Commentario Frontiniano ivi efpofto in compendio: la Pianta delle Terme le più cofpicue: del Foro Romano colle Contrade circonvicine: del Monte Capitolino: ed altre le più riguardevoli.

NEL SECONDO, E NEL TERZO
Gli Avanzi de' Monumenti Sepolcrali efiftenti in Roma, e nell' Agro Romano colle loro rifpettive piante, elevazioni, fezioni, vedute efterne ed interne: colla dimoftrazione de' farcofagi, ceppi, vafi cenerarj e unguentarj, baffirilievi, ftucchi, mufaici, ifcrizioni, e tutt' altro ch'è ftato in effi ritrovato: e colle loro indicazioni e fpiegazioni.

NEL QUARTO
I Ponti antichi di Roma che inoggi fono in effere, colle Veftigia dell' antica Ifola Tiberina, gli Avanzi de' Teatri, de' Portici, e di altri Monumenti, eziandio colle loro indicazioni e fpiegazioni.

TOMO PRIMO.

IN ROMA, MDCCLVI.
NELLA STAMPERIA DI ANGELO ROTILJ
NEL PALAZZO DE' MASSIMI.
CON LICENZA DE' SUPERIORI.

SI VENDONO IN ROMA DAI SIGNORI BOUCHARD, E GRAVIER MERCANTI LIBRAJ AL CORSO
PRESSO SAN MARCELLO.

Catalogue Number 31 [1]. VEDUTE DI ROMA

Title Page

VEDVTE DI ROMA
DISEGNATE ED INCISE
DA GIAMBATTISTA PIRANESI
ARCHITETTO VENEZ.

Catalogue Number 31 [2]. VEDUTE DI ROMA

Frontispiece

Catalogue Number 31 [3]. VEDUTE DI ROMA

St. Peter's with Forecourt and Colonnades.

Veduta della Basilica, e Piazza di S. Pietro in Vaticano

Catalogue Number 31 [4]. VEDUTE DI ROMA

St. Peter's. Interior, with the Nave.

Veduta interna della Basilica di S. Pietro in Vaticano.

Si vendono in Roma dai S.ri Bouchard e Gravier Mercanti Librarj al Corso presso S. Marcello.

Piranesi fecit

Catalogue Number 31 [5]. VEDUTE DI ROMA

St. Peter's, from the Piazza della Sagrestia.

VEDUTA DELL' ESTERNO DELLA GRAN BASILICA DI S. PIETRO IN VATICANO. Architettura di Michelangelo Buonarota. Questa fu eretta in parte sopra i fondamenti del Circo Neroniano. Pranci, Architetto fec.
teresi in piede l'Palazzo che un'tavole nella Torza di S. Pietro, e facevà centro sulla Spina del Circo Studb° 3. La, gran Cupola, nella cima della quale evvi la Palla di metallo, dentro cui vi capisono circa venti persone. 4. Monte Vaticano. 5. Avanzi di Colonne di Granito e marmo Pario, le quali pervenivano
l'Obbelisco i demolito da Neto V°   Pranci Scauro a'cui da Pietro nel palerta Roma viene dta Ponta di mano. A quali 16 e marmo

Catalogue Number 31 [6]. VEDUTE DI ROMA

S. Paolo Fuori delle Mura.

Veduta della Basilica di S. Paolo fuor delle mura, eretta da Costantino Magno. 1. *Laterali rustici della Basilica che dimostrano l'opera esterna del detto Imperadore.* 2. *Ornamenti, Musaici, e finestre fattovi dai successori Cesari, e ristaurati dai Sommi Pontefici.* 3. *Portico ultimamente aggiuntovi sotto il Pontificato di Benedetto XIII.* 4. *Porta Santa.* 5. *Parte Settentrionale della Basilica verso Roma, e Monti sotto de' quali è uno degl' ingressi delle Catacombe degli antichi Cristiani.*

Piranesi F.

Catalogue Number 31 [7]. VEDUTE DI ROMA

S. Paolo Fuori delle Mura. Interior.

Spaccato interno della Basilica di S. Paolo fuori delle Mura, eretta da Costantino Magno, divisa in cinque Navate co'sua Crociata. Ottanta Colonne di marmo greco venato di vario colore, qua'i trasportate dal Sepolcro di Adriano Imperatore, sostentano le Navate variando di grandezza, e lavoro della Navata di mezzo. Altre Colonne, dieci di Granito sono sparse per la Crociata; interno alla quale, come anco interno la Navata di mezzo cronologicamente disposti si veggono i Ritratti di tutti i Sommi Pontefici Romani con altre Pitture antiche ora quasi consumate dal tempo. Il Pavimento delle Navate è formato di rotti pezzi di marmo, levati dalle Rovine de'altri Edificii antichi.

Presso l'Autore a Strada Felice nel palazzo Tomati vicino alla Trinità de'monti, a paoli due e mezzo. Piranesi fecit

Catalogue Number 31 [8]. VEDUTE DI ROMA

S. Giovanni in Laterano. Main Facade with Palace and Scala Santa on the Right.

Veduta della Basilica di S. Giovanni Laterano

Architettura d' Aleßandro Gallilei

1. Cappella fabricata da Clemente XII Corßini
2. Palazzo fabricato da Sisto V ora Conßer. di Zitelle
3. Scala Santa

4. Guglia Egiziaca giacente
5. Muro della Città

Architettura d' Aleßandro Gallilei

Presso l'Autore a Strada Felice nel Palazzo Tomati vicino alla Trinità de' monti a' paoli due e mezzo

Piranesi del Scul

Catalogue Number 31 [9]. VEDUTE DI ROMA

S. Maria Maggiore with the Column from the Basilica of Constantine in the Foreground.

Veduta della Basilica di S.ᵃ Maria Maggiore con le due Fabbriche laterali di detta Basilica

1. Colonna antica, del Tempio della Pace,   La Facciata di mezzo Architettura del Cav.ʳ Ferdinando Fuga.   Pone l'osservatore nel Palazzo Romani vicino alla Trinità de' Monti, A poche ore a marza.
quivi eretta da Paolo V.
2. Ospitale di S. Antonio Abate.   Piranesi Fel. Sc.

Catalogue Number 31 [10]. VEDUTE DI ROMA

S. Maria Maggiore, with the Obelisk in the Piazza dell' Esquilino.

Veduta della Facciata di dietro della Basilica di S. Maria Maggiore

1. Cappella di Sisto V.   2 Cappella di Paolo V.   3 Obelisco ritrovato fra le rovine del Mausoleo d'Augusto, e fatto quivi trasportare ed erigere da Sisto V.   4. Villa Montalto   Giov. Battista Piranesi Architetto dis dis.

Catalogue Number 31 [*11*]. VEDUTE DI ROMA

S. Croce in Gerusalemme.

Veduta della Facciata della Basilica di S. Croce in Gerusalemme

1. Monastero de' Monaci Cisterciensi.   2. Muro moderno fabbricato sulle rovine dell'Anfiteatro Castrense.   3. Avanzi del Tempio della Speranza Vecchia.   Giovan Battista Piranesi Architetto dis. ed inc.

Catalogue Number 31 [*12*]. VEDUTE DI ROMA

S. Lorenzo Fuori delle Mura.

Veduta della Basilica di S. Lorenzo fuor delle mura

1. Via Tiburtina.   Presso l'Autore, poco lontano a mezza   Francesi

Catalogue Number 31 [*14*]. VEDUTE DI ROMA

The Piazza del Popolo.

Veduta della Piazza del Popolo

Catalogue Number 31 [*15*]. VEDUTE DI ROMA

The Piazza del Quirinale, with the Statues of the Horse Tamers in Side View.

Veduta della Piazza di Monte Cavallo

1. Palazzo Pontificio   Palazzo della Famiglia Pontificia   opere di Prasitelle, e Fidia Scultori Greci   Piranesi del. et comp.
2. Palazzo della Famiglia Pontificia   4. Quartiere de Soldati, e Scuderia Pontificia
3. Statue Colossali rappresentanti Alessandro che doma il Bucefalo   5. Palazzo Rospigliosi   Presso l'Autore a Strada Felice vicino la Trinità de' monti Appresso il mo

Catalogue Number 31 [*16*]. VEDUTE DI ROMA

The Piazza Navona, with S. Agnese on the Right.

Veduta di Piazza Navona sopra le rovine del Circo Agonale

1. S.ª Agnese
2. Palazzo Panfili
3. Fontana con Guglia Egizziaca archit.ª di Bernini
4. S. Giacomo de Spagnoli
5. Fontana Architettura di Michelangelo
6. Prangli Sala....
7. Fontana incontro al Palazzo Panfili

Preso l'intiero a Oriente nel Palazzo Bonati vicino alla Fonte de mani Apollinare.

Catalogue Number 31 [*17*]. VEDUTE DI ROMA

The Piazza della Rotonda, with the Pantheon and Obelisk.

Veduta della Piazza della Rotonda

1. Pantheon fabbricato da Marco Agrippa ogni i S.Maria ad Martyres
2. Fontana con Guglia Egiziaca architettura di Filippo Barromini.
3. S.Filippo Barromini.
3. Pescaria
4. Palazzo Crescenzi
Posta Pontra e Bottila nel Palazzo Tonati vicino alla Penta di mezo Sparlic in bra.
Piranesi del. sc.

Catalogue Number 31 [*18*]. VEDUTE DI ROMA

The Piazza di Spagna.

Veduta di Piazza di Spagna.

1. Fontana, detta la Barcaccia, Architettura del Cav. Bernino. 2. Scalinata, che conduce sul monte Pincio. 3. Chiesa col Monastero della SS. Trinità de' monti officiata dai Frati Minimi di S. Francesco di Paola della Nazione Franzese. 4. Strada del Babuino, che và alla Porta del Popolo. 5. Obelisco nella Piazza del Popolo.

Piranesi Archit. fec.

Presso l'Autore a Strada Felice nel palazzo Tomati vicino alla Trinità de' monti. A paoli due e mezzo.

Catalogue Number 31 [*19*]. VEDUTE DI ROMA

The Fontana di Trevi. Side View.

Veduta della vasta Fontana di Trevi anticamente detta l'Acqua Vergine.
Architettura di Nicola Salvi.

Piranesi del. Scolp.

Presso l'Autore a Strada Felice nel Palazzo Tomati vicino alla Trinità de' monti. Apoli due e mezzo.

Catalogue Number 31 [20]. VEDUTE DI ROMA

The Fontana dell' Acqua Felice.

SIXTVS•PONTIF•MAXIMVS
PICENVS
AQVAM•EX•AGRO•COLVMNAE•PROLACVM
S•QVAR•ENES•CEP•EPTACVLT
AQVA•M•ENES•CEP•EPTACVLT
VILIA•INVOSO•AXII•ADPONTED•VII
MDXX•A•C•ANOMINE•ANTEPONTED•VII
MIERVE•A•DE•NOMINE
SIXTVS•PONTAN••SOVII•I•SOVII•I•MDXXXVII•MDXXXVII

Veduta del Castello dell'Acqua Felice
presso le Terme Diocleziane,   *e Chiesa di S.Maria della Vittoria*

Catalogue Number 31 [*21*]. VEDUTE DI ROMA

The Fontana dell' Acqua Paola.

PAVLVS·QVINTVS·PONTIFEX·MAXIMVS
AQVAM·IN·AGRO·BRACCIANENSI·SALVBERRIMIS·E·FONTIBVS·COLLECTAM
VETERIBVS·AQVAE·ALSIETINAE·DVCTIBVS·RESTITVTIS
NOVISQVE·ADDITIS
XXXV·AB·MILLIARIO·DVXIT

Veduta del Castello dell' Acqua Paola sul Monte Aureo
1. Casino Farnese. 2. Basilica di S. Pietro in Vaticano. 3. Casino e
Orto Botanico. 4. Avanzo delle Mura urbane dell' Imperadore Aureliano.
G.B. Piranesi Architetto

Catalogue Number 31 [22]. VEDUTE DI ROMA

The Palazzo della Consulta.

Veduta del Palazzo fabbricato sul Quirinale per le Segreterie de Brevi e della Sacra Consulta
Architettura del Cavalier Ferdinando Fuga

1. Corpo di Guardia de' Cavaleggieri.   2. Corpo di Guardia di Corazzieri.   3. Palazzo Apostolico.   4. Corpo di Guardia di Soldati Rossi.   5. Palazzo del Sig.r Principe Rospigliosi.   6. Monastero e Chiesa di
S. Maria Maddalena.   7. Porta Pia sulle Mura Urbane.

Gio. Battista Piranesi Architetto dis. e inc.

Catalogue Number 31 [23]. VEDUTE DI ROMA

The Palazzo di Monte Citorio.

1. Veduta della Gran Curia Innocenziana edificata sulle rovine dell'Anfiteatro di Statilio Tauro, che formano l'odierno Monte Citorio. 2. Residenza di Monsig. Tesorier Generale 4. Gran Sala dell'Udienza.
2. Residenza de' Prelati Luogotenenti dell'Uditorato. 6. Ufizij, e Cancellerie de' Notari del medesimo Uditorato. 7. Palazzo colle Segreterie e Cancellieri della Ren. Camera. 8. Piedistallo che sosteneva anticamente la Colonna dell'Antonino Pio. 3. Residenza di Monsig. Uditor Generale della Ren. Camera.
delle vicine Case de' Signori della Missione, fatto ultimamente erigere sulla piazza, dalla Santità di N.S. Benedetto XIV. 9. Piazza Colonna. 10. Colonna Antonina colle gesta di M. Aurelio per la vittoria de' Marcomanni. 11. Palazzo del Principe Chigi. 12. Palazzo Spada sulla via del Corso.

Piranesi F.

Catalogue Number 31 [24]. VEDUTE DI ROMA

The Palazzo dell'Accademia di Francia (The Palazzo Salviati).

VEDUTA, nella Via del Corso, DEL PALAZZO DELL'ACCADEMIA istituita da LUIGI XIV RE DI FRANCIA per i Nazionali Francesi studiosi della Pittura, Scultura, e Architettura; colla liberal permissione al Pubblico di eser-
citarvisi in tali arti per il comodo della esposizione quotidiana del Nudo, e dei Modelli delle più rare Statue ed altri Segni della Romana Magnificenza, si antichi, che moderni.   1. Stanze ove sono esposti i modelli della Colonna Trajana, Statue Eque-
stri, e Pedestri, Busti, e Bassirilievi.   2. Stanze per l'esposizione del Nudo.   3. Appartamento Regio ornato parimente di Modelli.   4. Appartamento del Signor Direttore.   5. Palazzo Panfili.   6. Via del Corso.   7. Porta del Popolo.
Presso l'Autore a Strada Felice vicino alla Trinità dei monti   Gio. Batta. Piranesi Architetto dis. inc.

Catalogue Number 31 [25]. VEDUTE DI ROMA

The Palazzo Barberini.

Piranesi f.

Veduta sul Monte Quirinale del Palazzo dell'Eccellentissima Casa Barberini, Architettura del Cav.r Bernino

1. Ponte levatoio, che dal vestibolo superiore di   2. Iscrizione dell'Arco di Claudio ridrovata fra le   3. Labro antico di granito, che serve alla   6. Obelisco Egizziaco, in trasporto dal Circo d'Elagabalo e come
l'ingresso al Secondo appartamento del Palazzo.   di sua rovine sulla Piazza di Sciarra,   Fontana del Vestibolo inferiore.   altri vogliono d'Aurelian, che rimanea fuori dell'odierna Porta Magg.e
    dicesi tante le Marmi reportate da questi Imperadori sopra i Brittanni.   4. Chiesa de' Cappuccini   5. Uno de' Portoni del Vestibolo, che serve alla   rispondente alla Piazza Barberini.

Catalogue Number 31 [26]. VEDUTE DI ROMA

The Palazzo Odescalchi.

Veduta del Palazzo Odescalchi

1. Palazzo Colonna. 2. Basilica de' SS. XII. Apostoli. 3. Convento de' PP. Minor. Conventuali. 4. Palazzo Muti. 5. Convento de' PP. Serviti di S. Marcello. 6. Piazza de' SS. Apostoli.

Presso l'Autore a Strada Felice nel palazzo Tomati vicino alla Trinità de' monti A paoli due e mezzo.

Gio. Batt. Piranesi Arch. F.

Catalogue Number 31 [27]. VEDUTE DI ROMA

The Harbour and Quay, Called the Ripa Grande.

Veduta del Porto di Ripa Grande

1. Dogana grande. 2. Dogana del passo. 3. Arsenale. 4. Granari dell'Annona. 5. Ospizio Apostolico di S. Michele, e Casa degl'Invalidi; di educazione nelle arti e correzione de' Fanciulli, e di condanna delle Donne delinquenti. 6. Avanzi di una delle pile dell'antico Ponte Sublicio già di Legno, e rifatto poscia di pietra da Emilio, e ristorato dai Cesari. 7. Avanzi delle Saline antiche, e de' muri de' tempi bassi falsamente supposti del detto Ponte Sublicio.

G.B. Piranesi Architetto fec.

Catalogue Number 31 [*28*]. VEDUTE DI ROMA

The Smaller Harbour, Called the Porto di Ripetta.

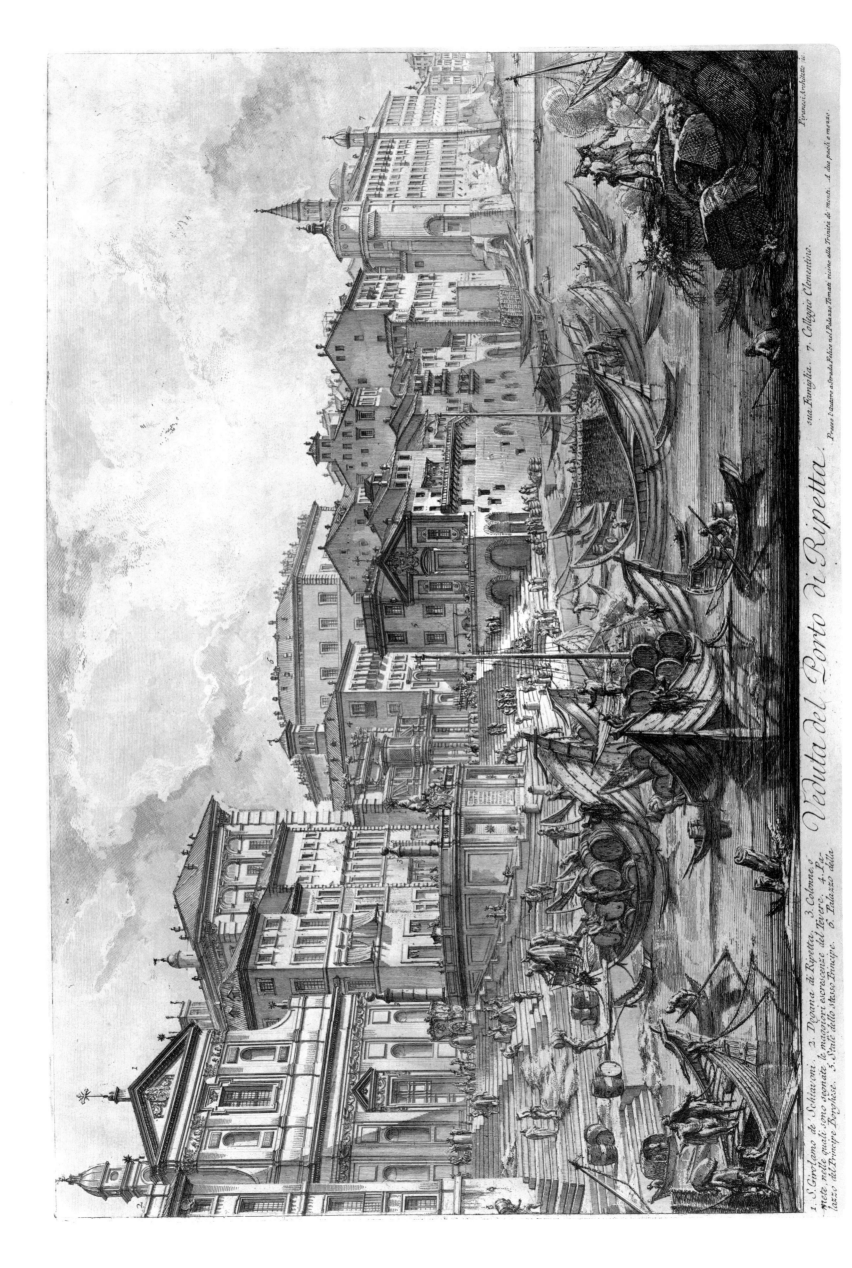

Veduta del Porto di Ripetta.

1. S. Girolamo de Schiavoni. 2. Dogana di Ripetta. 3. Colonne, o Mete, nelle quali sono segnate le maggiori escrescenze del Tevere. 4. Facciata del Principe Borghese. 5. Stalle della Stesso Principe. 6. Palazzo della sua Famiglia. 7. Colleggio Clementino.

Piranesi Architetto ...

Pesca l'acqua a strada Felice nel Palazzo Tomati vicino alla Trinità de' monti . A due paoli e mezzo.

Catalogue Number 31 [29]. VEDUTE DI ROMA

The Ponte and Castel S. Angelo.

Veduta del Ponte e Castello Sant'Angelo.

1. Avanzi del Sepolcro di Adriano Imp.re Da questo furono levate da Costantino Magno le Colonne della Basilica di S.Paolo fuori delle mura. Nella cima di esso era collocata la Pigna di metallo, dentro la quale stavano riposte le ceneri del medesimo Adriano: da quì, fu trasportata in tempo de Parenti, pur di me

tallo nel Giardino di Belvedere nel Vaticano. Questo Sepolcro poi fu ridotto in forma di Castello. 2. Basilica di S.Pietro in Vaticano. 3. Palazzo Pontificio. 4. Ospitale di S.Spirito. 5. Teatro di Tordinona. 6. Espurgo delle immondezze della Città. Presso l'antica strada Felice nel palazzo Tomacini vicino alla Trinità de'monti: A quali due a mano

Catalogue Number 31 [30]. VEDUTE DI ROMA

The Castel S. Angelo.

VEDUTA del Mausoleo d'Elio Adriano, ora chiamato Castello S. Angelo; nella parte opposta alla Facciata dinanzi al Castello. A Avanzo del Masso antico. B Copertura moderna di mattoni sopra l'antico Masso. C Bocche di Artiglieria collocata nel Corridojo, che gira all'intorno. D Loggia diametrale, opposta alla Facciata del Mausoleo. E Camerini per le persone riguardevoli. F Archivio. G Malvichio. H Angioli di metallo. I Baluardi tutti piantati dal Pontefice Alessandro VI. K Corridojo fabbricato parim. percosto dall'istesso; e polita fatto coprire da Urbano VIII. Ingele Corridojo esistente da gran numere di luoghi, e dal Palazzo Vaticano conduce sino dentro al Mastio. L Ponte levatore del Corridojo. M Polveriera. N Cordonati. O Recinto di Mura, e Baluardi, che circonda il Mastio. P Armeria. Q Mutazione per gli Uficiali, e Soldati. R Altra Polveriera. Piazza l'Autore a Urbale Salva vicino alla Fontana de'Monti A pochi sbair morani. Piranesi Archit. dis. inc.

Catalogue Number 31 [*31*]. VEDUTE DI ROMA

The Ponte Salario.

Veduta del Ponte Salario

Elce fù fabbricato sull' Aniene due miglia lontan da Roma, ed è fra i ponti antichi
Eloc fù fabbricato l'Aniene rimaro intero à nostri tempi. 2. Lapide di marmo nel pregio del ponte colla memoria di Narvete scolpita dalla parte interna. 2.3. Torricella dalla parte interna.

riormente. 4. Modelli usati nella costruzione dell' arco, e lasciatvi per comodo nè di lui, formati riscarci-
menti. 5. Cavo in cui era uno di detti modelli caduto 6. Archi fatti in difesa del Ponte dall' impeto dell' acqua
nelle escrecenze del Fiume. 7. Fiume Aniene, ovvero Teverone. 8. Via Salaria. 9. Avanzo di antico Sepolcro convertiti
dei, fabbricati moderni.

Catalogue Number 31 [*32*]. VEDUTE DI ROMA

The Hadrianeum (once used as a Customs House) in the Piazza di Pietra.

Veduta della Dogana di Terra a Piazza di Pietra

Questa fù fabbricata sulle rovine del Tempio di M. Aurelio
Antonino Pio nel suo Foro.
1. Avanzo di colonne rimaste, oggi messo
interrate nella nuova Fabbrica.
2. Architrave antico ristorato.
3. Cornicione, ed Ordine Attico nuovamente rifatto.

4. Abitazione moderna.
5. Collegio Bergamasco.
6. Quartiere de' Soldati.
7. Strada che va al Corso.

Piranesi Architetto fec.

Presso l'Autore a Strada Felice nel palazzo Tomati vicino alla Trinità dè monti. A paoli due e mezzo.

Catalogue Number 31 [*33*]. VEDUTE DI ROMA

The Theatre of Marcellus.

TEATRO DI MARCELLO.

Questo fu fabricato da Augusto, e dedicato a Marcello suo Nipote.   2. Capella di S. Maria in Campitelli.   Piranesi Architetto, fec.
1. Palazzo Orsini restaurato da Baldassare da Siena Architetto.   Prende l'autore questa strada Polio pel Palazzo Tomati vicino alla Trinità de'monti a'due passi e mezzo.

Catalogue Number 31 [34]. VEDUTE DI ROMA

The Fontana dell' Acqua Giulia.

Veduta dell'avanzo del Castello, che prendendo una porzione dell'Acqua Giulia dal Condotto principale, parte ne diffondeva in una magnifica fontana che gli era aderente, è decorata da M. Agrippa fra gli altri ornamenti de Trofei d'Augusto che ora si vedono sul Campidoglio, e parte ne tramandava per via del Monte Celio. 1. Luogo, donde furon tolti i detti Trofei. 2. Porzione di barbacani rifatta dai moderni. 3. Diramazioni dello speco del Castello, le quali tramandavano l'acqua nella fontana, e per il Celio. 4. Muri, e Casino moderni. 5. Villa Palombara.

Catalogue Number 31 [35]. VEDUTE DI ROMA

The Pyramid of Caius Cestius, with the Porta S. Paolo and Adjoining Road.

1. Porta S. Paolo
2. Mura di Roma

Veduta del Sepolcro di Cajo Cestio

Presso l'Autore a Strada Felice nel Palazzo Tomati vicino alla Trinità de'monti. A paoli due e mezzo

Catalogue Number 31 [36]. VEDUTE DI ROMA

The Pyramid of Caius Cestius.

Piramide di C. Cestio

1. Terreno sgombrato d'in torno alla Piramide sotto il
Pontificato d' Alessandro VII. 2. Porta aperta di quel
tempo nella Piramide. 3. Colonne ritrovate nella
.... escavata nell' antica positura. 4. Mu-
.... di Roma. 5. Torre della Porta di
S. Paolo.

Catalogue Number 31 [37]. VEDUTE DI ROMA

S. Costanza (erroneously called Temple of Bacchus).

Piranesi Architetto fec.

VEDUTA INTERNA DEL SEPOLCRO DI S. COSTANZA, FABBRICATO DA
COSTANTINO MAGNO, ED ERRONEAMENTE DETTO IL TEMPIO DI
BACCO. INOGGI CHIESA DELLA MEDESIMA SANTA.

1. Colonne, basi, capitelli di grandezza e ornamenti di varia: 2. Musaici antichi. 3. Finestre
di, tutti da diversi edifizi. 2. Musaici antichi. 3. Finestre
antiche. 4. Candelieri antichi di marmo. 5. Pitture moderne. 6. Urna
di Porfido tutta d'un pezzo lunga pal. 11. alta p. 5. 10. larga 6.3. Il coperchio alto 3.3.

Presso l'autore a strada Felice vicino alla Trinità de' Monti. A paoli dui e mezzo.

Catalogue Number 31 [*38*]. VEDUTE DI ROMA

The Capitol and the Steps of S. Maria in Aracoeli.

Veduta del Romano Campidoglio con Scalinata, che và alla Chiesa d'Aracli
Architettura di Michelangelo Bonaroti

1. Abitazione del Senator Romano.
2. Museo ove si conservano le Statue antiche.
3. Palazzo de Conservatori.
4. Statua equestre di Marco Aurelio di metallo Corintio.

Preso havere a lenta Fatia ed Palazzo Senato vicino alla Trinità di Roma.

5. Statue Colossali antiche di Castor, e Polluce.
6. Trofei d'Augusto, volgarmente detti di Mario.
7. Colonne Miliaria aurea.
8. Leonessa di marmo Egizia.

Appresso dove a mano.

Piranesi Del. Sol.

Catalogue Number 31 [39]. VEDUTE DI ROMA

The Capitol, seen from the Side of the Central Steps.

Veduta del Campidoglio di fianco

1. Statua equestre di M. Aurelio nella già Campidolina. 2. Palazzo, ò
Casa, ù detta il Senatore di Roma. 3. Palazzo degli Eccelsi Conservatori di Roma.
4. Museo Capitolino. 5. Trofei d'Augusto, volgarmente detti di Mario.
6. 7. Colossi di Caspe, e Lucio, sotto il simbolo di Castore, e Polluce.
8. 9. Statue di Costantino Magno. 10. Colonna milliaria. 11. Palazzo Caffarelli.

Catalogue Number 31 [40]. VEDUTE DI ROMA

The Forum Romanum, or Campo Vaccino, from the Capitol.

Veduta di Campo Vaccino

1. Vestigie del Tempio di Giove Tonante
2. Tempio di Antonino, e Faustina
3. Tempio di Romolo, e Remo, ora S. Cosma e Dam.i
4. S. Francesca Romana
5. Arco di Tito
6. Vestigie del Palazzo de' Cesari nel Palatino
7. Colonne del Tempio di Giove Statore
8. Miraglioni dei Rostri
9. Avanzi del Palatino della Casa aurea

1. Tempio d'Antonino, e Faustina
2. Tempio del Tempio della Concordia
3. Arco di Settimio Severo
4. Antico Erario sotto il Adriano

10. Colosseo
11. Avanzo di due Trichini della detta Casa aurea
12. Avanzo del Palatino della Casa aurea di Nerone
13. Vestigie delle Terme di Tito

Piranesi del Ecc.

Posto l'autore a Strada Felice nel palazzo Tomati vicino alla Trinità de' monti, a paoli due a mezzo.

Catalogue Number 31 [*41*]. VEDUTE DI ROMA

A Corner of the Forum Romanum with the Temple of Castor and Pollux in Foreground Left.

Veduta del Sito, ov'era l'antico Foro Romano.

1. Luogo, ove erano situati i Rostri. 2. Altro luogo, ov'e
Basilica in questo luogo in questo era riunpo privati Romele.
3. S. Teodoro. 4. Monte Palatino con Vestigii
del'Edificio di Cesare. 6. Colonne del Tempio di Giove Statore.

7. Vacca di Granito orientale tutta d'un pezzo di extraordinaria, in qual'è Sito
avavi la voragine di Curezio. 8. Monte Aventino. 9. Acqua, che scorre nella Cloaca massima.
Tutta questa parte memorabile nella Storia Romana, particolarm. per li Rostri, da quali si riper
Roma portata qui dal Tevere posciato al Foro superiore sui Cittadini Romani.
sare da Marcantonio, la testa e mani, di Cicerone, ec. e Sepolcro posto su i superiormo i Capi dotti vestri come fu la Voce inammorata olle.

Catalogue Number 31 [42]. VEDUTE DI ROMA

The Forum of Augustus (erroneously called Forum of Nerva).

Veduta degli avanzi del **Foro di Nerva**

1. *Avanzo della Curia del Foro, occupata inoggi dalla Chiesa, e dal Monastero della Religiose* — *recinto del Foro. 5 Finestre della stessa Chiesa, di maniera gotica, aperte nel detto recinto.*
2. *dell'annunziata a una delle chiese principali, colocavano l'ingresso nel Foro, dato inoggi Chiesa di S. Urbani* — *6 Case fabbricate ne' tempi bassi di pertinenza del medesimo Monastero.*
3. *Archi inferiori che pavimento adorno l'ingresso nel Foro. 4 Porta della predetta Chiesa, aperta nell'antico* — *7 Convento e Chiese de' PP. di S. Quirico.*

Presso l'Autore a Strada Felice vid Palazzo Tomati vicino alla Trinità de' monti. Annidua a mezzo. — *Gio. Batt. Piranesi disegnò, ed incise*

Catalogue Number 31 [*43*]. VEDUTE DI ROMA

Roman Arches at the Church of SS. Giovanni e Paolo (formerly called the Curia Hostilia).

VEDUTA DEL PIANO SUPERIORE DEL SERRAGLIO DELLE FIERE FABBRICATO DA DOMIZIANO A USO DELL'ANFITEATRO FLAVIO, E VOLGARMENTE DETTO LA CURIA OSTILIA

Al primo piano di questa gran fabbrica rimane interrata nelle rovine, che inoggi uguagliano il piano di Roma, è dagli scavi fattivi, è trovato parimente composto di grossi macigni di travertino.   A Scavi, ove si appoggiavano i muri di tavolezza che serravano gli archi.   B Muri de' tempi Bassi: Sopra di questi Archi s'fabbricato il Campanile e Convento de'Padri della Mensione di SS. Giovanni, l'acto

Presso l'Autore a Strada Felice vicino alla Trinità de' monti A paoli due e mezzo.

Catalogue Number 31 [44]. VEDUTE DI ROMA

The Temple of Vespasian.

Veduta del Tempio di Giove Tonante

Catalogue Number 31 [45]. VEDUTE DI ROMA

The Basilica of Constantine.

VEDUTA DEGLI AVANZI DEL TABLINO DELLA CASA AUREA DI NERONE, DETTI VOLGARMENTE IL TEMPIO DELLA PACE

1. Di qui fu trasportata da Paolo V. la gran Colonna che si vede innalzata nella Piazza di S. Maria Maggiore.   2. Muri, e piloni che reggevano la parte opposta del Tablino.   3. Nicchie per le Statue degli uomini illustri.
Presso l'Autore a Strada Felice vicino alla Trinità de' monti.   A paoli due e mezzo.

Catalogue Number 31 [46]. VEDUTE DI ROMA

The So-called Temple of Fortuna Virilis (now Church of S. Maria Egiziaca).

Piranesi Architetto fece.

Veduta del Tempio della Fortuna virile.

Oggi S. Maria Egiziaca degli Armeni. 1. Residui d'un antico   a questo Tempio sbocca nel Tevere la Cloaca massima.
Fabrica chiamata dal Volgo la Casa di Pilato. 2. Ospizio della   4. S. Maria in Cosmedin detta la Scola Greca. 5. Monte Aventino.
Nazione Armena. 3. Tempio di Vesta: oggi S. Maria del Sole, vicino   Passeggiatore a Benedettini nel palazzo Senatori suora alla Trinità de' monti. A questi due e mezza   sotto al quale si vedono i vestigj della Spelonca di Caco.

Catalogue Number 31 [47], VEDUTE DI ROMA

The Temple of Fortunus (?) (the Round Temple Near S. Maria in Cosmedin).

Veduta del Tempio di Cibele a Piazza della Bocca della Verità.

Presso l'Autore a Strada Felice vicino alla Trinità de'monti: al prezzo di un paolo e mezzo

Catalogue Number 31 [*48*]. VEDUTE DI ROMA

The So-called Temple of Bacchus, Now the Church of S. Urban.

Veduta del Tempio di Bacco, in oggi Chiesa di S. Urbano, distante due miglia da Roma fuori della Porta di S. Sebastiano. Ecco e'l più intero di questa, forma, che cia rimaco a Roma ai giorni nostri, e'il più antico che ne abbiamo. La rit. [...] ringraziamo [...] ECITAI. ΔΙΟΝΥϹΟΥ. ΑΠΡΟΝΙΑΝΟϹ.ΙΕΡΟΦΑΝΤΗϹ: Ara di Bacco, Approniano Sacerdote. 1. Muri, fra gl'Intercolonny del Pronao, e barbacani [...] nell'esterne che nell'interno. 2. Chiari, delle catene di ferro impiegatevi per lo stesso fine. 3. Avanzo dell'antica cara dell'Edifizio [...] fatti da Urbano VIII per riparar la rovina del Tem[pio] [...] Gio. Bat. Piranesi Arch. F.

Catalogue Number 31 [*49*]. VEDUTE DI ROMA

The Temple of Antoninus and Faustina.

Veduta del Tempio di Antonino e Faustina in Campo Vaccino

Piranesi Architetto fece

1. S. Lorenzo in Miranda di Speziali

Catalogue Number 31 [50]. VEDUTE DI ROMA

The Temple of Venus and Roma (erroneously called Temple of Sol and Luna).

Veduta degli avanzi di due Triclinj, che appartenevano alla Casa aurea di Nerone, presi erroneamente per i Templi del Sole, e della Luna, o d'Iside, e Seraphide. 1. Avanzo del Triclinio a uso dell'estate. 2. Avanzo dell'altro a uso dell'inverno. Questi rimangono nel Giardino de' PP. di S. Francesca Romana in Campo Vaccino.

Piranesi Carce ... Fecit nel Palazzo ... Trinità de' Monti ... G. B. Piranesi Archit. incise

Catalogue Number 31 [*51*]. VEDUTE DI ROMA

Trajan's Column.

1. *Bucca fatta scavare da Sisto V. con recinto di muro, e Scala, che discende al piano della Colonna.*
2. *Chiesa del Nome di Maria.*
3. *Palazzo Bonelli*

Colonna Trajana

Piranesi fecit

Presso l'Autore a Strada Felice nel Palazzo Tomati vicino alla Trinità de'monti A paoli due e mezzo

Catalogue Number 31 [52]. VEDUTE DI ROMA

The Column of Marcus Aurelius.

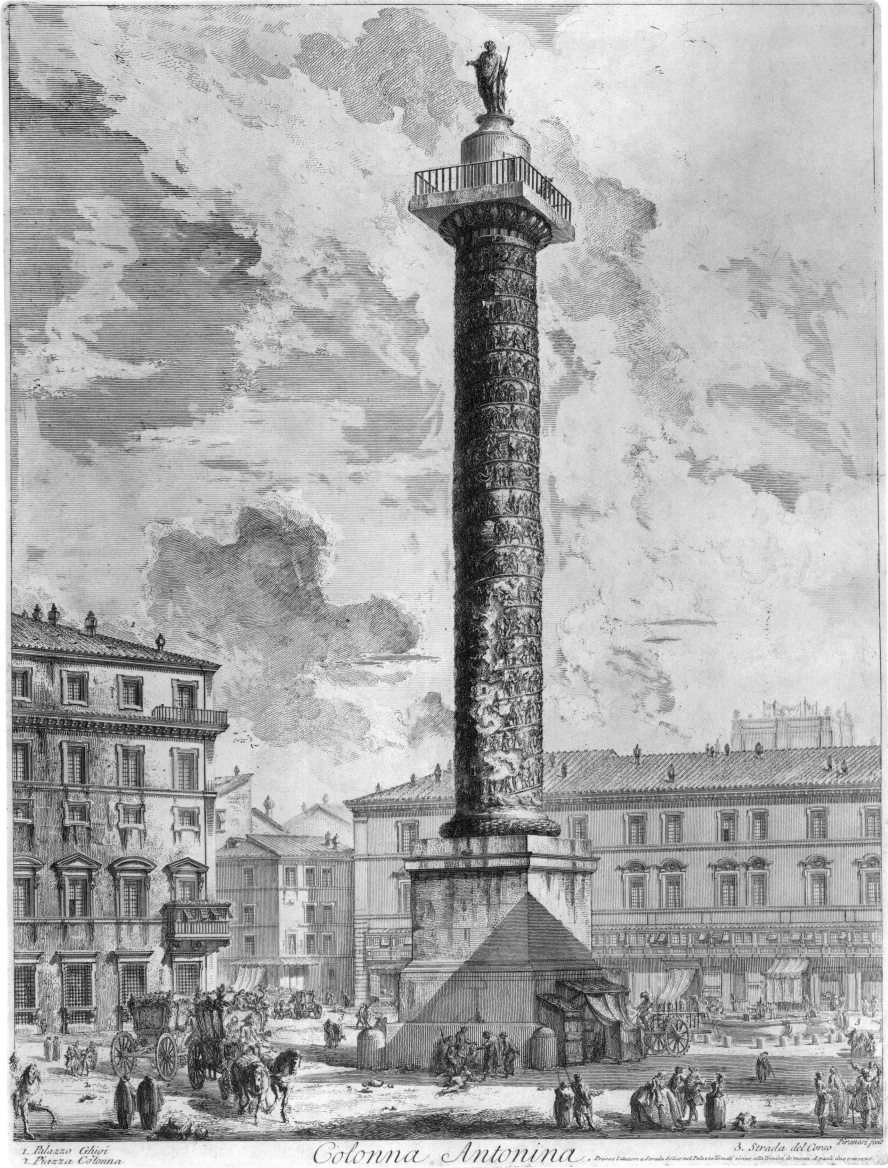

1. *Palazzo Ghigi*
2. *Piazza Colonna*

3. *Strada del Corso*

Piranesi fecit

Colonna Antonina . Presso l'Autore a Strada Felice nel Palazzo Tomati vicino alla Trinità de'monti. A paoli due e mezzo

Catalogue Number 31 [53]. VEDUTE DI ROMA

The Egyptian Obelisk in the Piazza di S. Giovanni Laterano.

Piranesi Architetto fec.

OBELISCO EGIZIO

Questo fù eretto da Sisto V. nella Piazza di S. Gio. Laterano.
1. Palazzo fabricato da Sisto V. ora Conservatorio di Zitelle.
2. Scala Santa.
3. Rovine di Acquedotti antichi.

Catalogue Number 31 [54]. VEDUTE DI ROMA

The Arch of Septimius Severus with the Church of S. Martina.

Arco di Settimio Severo.

1. Erario antico, o come altri, Tempio di Saturno, oggi S. Adriano. 2. S. Martina. 6. Chiesa dell'Aracceli fabbricata sopra i fondamenti del Tempio di Giove Capitolino.
architettato da Pietro da Cortona. Chiesa dell'Academia, detta di S. Luca. 3. S. Luca. 7. Colonna rimasta in piedi, creduta del Ponte, che fece fare l'Imperatore Cutigola per passare
il co quivero alcun framento nel quale sono stati posti i SS. Pietro, e Paolo. Sopra questo si vede eretta dal Palatino al Campidoglio.
la Chiesa di S. Giuseppe. 4. Salita che porta al Campidoglio. 5. Abitazione del Senatore Romano. Nel mezzo di questo pazava a l'antica Via sacra che portava i Trionfi al Campid.
Piranesi Architetto fec.

Catalogue Number 31 [55]. VEDUTE DI ROMA

The Arch of Titus.

Veduta dell' Arco di Tito

Eretto questo Imperadore dopo la di lui morte in memoria della distruzione di
Gerosolima, e luoghi, e oppojsito della maggior parte de' suoi ornamenti. A. Bafsirilievi indi-
canti il di lui trionfo, adornato colle spoglie del Tempio di Salomone. B. Apoteosi dello

stefso Cesare, espressa in un' Aquila che lo colleva al Cielo. C. Orti Farneciani.
D. Chiesa di S. Sebastiano. E. Polveriere. F. Rovine della Casa Augustana sul Palatino.
G. Strada che conduce a S. Bonaventura.   Gio. Batta. Piranesi Architetto diseg. e incise

Prefso l'autore a Strada Felice vicino alla Trinità de'monti. A paoli due e mezzo.

Catalogue Number 31 [56]. VEDUTE DI ROMA

The Arch of Constantine and the Colosseum.

Veduta dell' Arco di Costantino, e dell' Anfiteatro Flavio detto il Colosseo

1. Meta Sudante.
2. Radici del Palatino.
3. Vestigie delle Terme di Tito.
4. Radici dell' Esquilino.

Presso l'Autore a Strada Felice vicino alla Trinità de' monti. A paoli due e mezzo.

Piranesi del Scolp.

Catalogue Number 31 [*58*]. VEDUTE DI ROMA

The Portico of Octavia: the Entrance Porch. Exterior.

Veduta dell'Atrio del Portico di Ottavia.

1. S. Angelo in Pescaria.   2. Interno dell'Atrio.   Ciascun de' quali in ispezie in piedi, un pezzo di marmi,

3. Tirelloni, di marmi, che s'ornano,   Alizi, hoyra;   intagliato di un Aquila in basso rilevo.   4. Pitture moderne.

Presso l'Autore a Strada Felice vicino alla Trinità de' monti. A paoli due e mezzo.

Piranesi Architetto fec.

Catalogue Number 31 [59]. VEDUTE DI ROMA

The Portico of Octavia: the Entrance Porch. Interior.

Veduta interna dell'Atrio del Portico di Ottavia.

1. Due Frontespizi interiori del detto Portico. 2. Arco, che sostiene il Frontespizio fatto posteriormente da Settimio Severo, come i'indicava nella Iscrizione delle mori, Architett: jm. reggevano. 3. Colonne inferiori all'Atrio molto coperte nel muro con altri avanti nelle cantine, le quali sostenevano i lati del Portico: ogni Boscaria.

Catalogue Number 31 [60]. VEDUTE DI ROMA

The Pantheon. Exterior.

MAGRIPPALF COS TERTIVM FECIT

Veduta del Pantheon d'Agrippa oggi Chiesa di S. Maria ad Martyres

Catalogue Number 31 [61]. VEDUTE DI ROMA

The Temple of the Sibyl, Tivoli, with another Temple right, once used as Church of S. Giorgio.

Veduta del tempio della Sibilla in Tivoli

Catalogue Number 31 [62]. VEDUTE DI ROMA

The Temple of the Sibyl, Tivoli: the broken side of the Colonnade.

ALTRA VEDUTA DEL TEMPIO DELLA SIBILLA IN TIVOLI

Piranesi F.

Catalogue Number 31 [63]. VEDUTE DI ROMA

The Temple of the Sibyl, Tivoli.

EGELIOE

Altra Veduta del
tempio della Sibilla
in Tivoli

1 Sustruzioni dell' aja del
tempio dalla parte della
cascata del Teverone.
2 Parte del Tempio sup=
posto d'Albunea.

Piranesi F.

The Catalogue

Catalogue Number 1. TAVOLA P'MA (Drawing 1).

Title Page of Presentation Drawings Embodying Proposals for a New Sanctuary of S. Giovanni in Laterano, Rome

As noted by Felice Stampfle in her catalogue of Piranesi drawings in the Pierpont Morgan Library (*An Exhibition of Drawings*, 1949, Number 55; see her Numbers 56–58 for other drawings for the S. Giovanni in Laterano project), Piranesi mentions his project for the Lateran in the foreword of his *Diverse maniere d'adornare i cammini*, 1767. Addressed to the same Cardinal G. B. Rezzonico to whom the artist presented these drawings, he pointedly notes "l' approvazione di cui avete onorato, e i disegni impostimi dal Santissimo Padre [Clement XIII] compimento della Basilica Lateranense . . ."

Of the seven plans included in this series (see *Catalogue Numbers 4, 6, 7, 11, 13, 16*), this plan is not only closest to *Catalogue Number 4*, but they both represent the least ambitious of the several schemes. In both, the presbytery for the Pope, as Bishop of Rome, is at the head of the apse, and is preceded by an *esedra* — or forechoir — flanked to either side by the choir. The transept would be left essentially unchanged.

The motif of the eagle in the vignette occurs constantly throughout the series. But the artist avoids using the double eagle of the Rezzonico crest in favor of a more flamboyant creature.

Pen and gray ink over pencil, with inscriptions, vignette, and ruled border in brown ink.

WATERMARK: ₽

H. 35″ (889 mm.) W. 22⅜″ (561 mm.)

CONDITION: Sealing wax stains in four corners and in center show through paper from back.

TOP: *Pianta della Tribuna, del Presbiterio, e dell' Esedra della Basilica Lateranense, immaginati a seconda della gran Nave.*

CENTER: *Varj Disegni fatti d'ordine della Santità di Nostro Signore* PAPA CLEMENTE XIII *nel'anno 1764. dal Cav. RE Giovambatista Piranesi Arch.to pe'l compimento della nuova Basilica Lateranense: presentati dal medesimo Cav. RE nell'anno 1767. a S.E. Monsignor D. Giovambatista Rezzonico Nipote e Maggior-dome della Santita Sua.*

BOTTOM: An eagle with wings spread, garlands, and a scale in Roman feet, in Piranesi's hand. In the banderole, the legend for the plan of the west, or choir, project. *1. Presbiterio elevato due gradi di più della Esedra. 2. Esedra al pari della Crociata di architettura corrispondente a qu . . . della gran Nave. 3. Coro de' Musici di architettura corrispondente a quella de' nicchj d . . . H. Apostoli che girano intorno alla gran Nave. 4. Scale per salire al coro de' Musici. 5. Scale per salire alle stanze, o conditorj delle Reliquie. 6. Atrio, ed ingresso direntano della Basilica. 7. Atrio consimile, che communica con la Basilica, e con l'andito della Sagrestia. 8. Coro d'inverno de' Canonici. 9. Cappella del Presepio. Le altre parti si dichiareranne nelle loro respettivo elevazioni.*

Catalogue Number 2. TAVOLA SEC.ᴰᴬ(Drawing 2).

Cross Section Showing West Wall of Transept and View into Sanctuary

Although no legend for the numbers on the elevation is given, and the numbers are not collated with those of the plan on the Title Page, this drawing belongs with *Catalogue Number 1*. Numbers 2 and 12 on the elevation indicate the doors, leading to the vestibules, which were designed by Piranesi in the style of Borromini's reconstruction of the nave; in the plan, numbers 6 and 7 indicate *gl'ingressi deretani*.

The western wall of the transept (the liturgical east because the orientation of the Lateran is reversed) is otherwise unchanged, belonging to the papacy of Clement VIII (1597-1601) — the medieval fabric of the transept was then altered by Giacomo della Porta and Mannerist fresco and stucco work added. The central section of this transept wall is also transcribed in *Catalogue Numbers 4 and 7*.

Pen and gray ink, heightened by Piranesi with brown ink in altar frame, papal arms and garland of arch. Ruled border in brown ink.

INSCRIBED: (in brown ink, lower right) *Cav.ᴿ G. B. Piranesi fece.*

WATERMARK: ₽

H. 21¾″ (553 mm.) W. 33⅝″ (855 mm.)

CONDITION: Sealing wax stains in four corners and in center show through paper from back. Bottom left corner has been torn and repaired with reinforcement on back of sheet; top edge also reinforced.

TOP: *Elevazione ortografica, o sia Fronte della Tribuna e degl'ingressi deretani della Basilica Lateranense.* And the following note: *I numeri dall'uno fino al dodici circoscrivono l'opera da farsi per gl'ingressi deretani, e per la Tribuna.*

ON BANDEROLE AT TOP OF PAPAL CREST: CLEMENS XIII. PONT. MAX. A. VI. [1764]. ON TABLET OVER DOOR TO EACH SIDE OF CHANCEL (i.e., *gl'ingressi deretani*): *CLEMENS XIII. p.m.* in brown ink.

BOTTOM: Scale in Roman feet marked off on a ruler, with ribbons and the inscription: *Scala di Palma Romani CXX.*

Catalogue Number 3. TAVOLA TERZA (Drawing 3).

Longitudinal Section Showing South Wall of Sanctuary, with Transept and Beginning of Nave

This longitudinal section transcribes three bays of Francesco Borromini's nave reconstruction on the left, as well as the south transept wall with Cavaliere d'Arpino's fresco of the Ascension, which dates from Clement VIII's reign — both extant today.

The sanctuary proposal belongs with *Catalogue Numbers 1 and 2*. It is very close to the smaller longitudinal section of the same wall in The Pierpont Morgan Library drawing first published by Stampfle (*An Exhibition of Drawings*, Number 56; see also Fischer, pp. 209ff. and figure 5; and Bean and Stampfle, Number 231).

The south wall of nave and transept are also transcribed in *Catalogue Numbers 5, 8, and 15*, the north wall in *Catalogue Number 17*.

Pen and gray ink, heightened by Piranesi with brown ink in vignette at top, in garland insets, oval window frames, reliefs, and in ⊛ monogram in frieze. Ruled border in brown ink.

INSCRIBED: (in brown ink, lower right) *Cav.^R G. B. Piranesi fece.*

WATERMARK: ₽

H. 21¹⁵/₁₆″ (557 mm.) W. 35½″ (902 mm.)

CONDITION: Remains of sealing wax on back in corners, center, and top center; water stain in lower left corner.

TOP, ON LARGE BANDEROLE: *Sezione ortografica di fianc[o] della Tribuna, del Presbiterio, e dell'Esedra della Basilica Lateranens[e] immaginati con architettura corrispondente a quella della gran Nave.* An eagle, with wings spread, holds in its claws a ruler marked off in Roman feet and a pen; a garland is formed of a tasselled rope.

Catalogue Number 4. TAVOLA QUARTA (Drawing 4).

Plan and View of Sanctuary from the Transept

The proposal presented in this drawing differs from the one discussed above only in detail: the articulation of the apse wall, the more austere treatment of the vault, the decorative variations of the lateral doors.

Pen and gray ink, heightened by Piranesi with brown ink in central area of elevation. Ruled border in brown ink.

INSCRIBED: (in brown ink, lower right) *Cav.^R G. B. Piranesi fece.*

WATERMARK: ₽

H. 34¹⁵/₁₆″ (887 mm.) W. 22¹/₁₆″ (560 mm.)

CONDITION: Badly abraded in central area of elevation. Remains of sealing wax on back at corners and in the center. Bottom border smudged by water stains.

TOP, ABOVE PLAN: *Pianta della Tribuna, del Presbiterio, e dell'Esedra della Basilica Lateranense immaginati secondo l'architettura della gran Nave.* All the parts of the plan are labelled.

CENTER, ABOVE THE CORRESPONDING ELEVATION: *Elevazione ortografica, o sia Fronte della stessa Tribuna & degli atrj notati nella Pianta.* And the following note: *I numeri dall'uno fino al dodici circoscrivono l'opera da farsi per la Tribuna, e per gli Atrj.*

BOTTOM: A wooden plaque with a hole at each end, through which a garland is threaded. Within the plaque, the scale is given in *Palmi Romani.*

Catalogue Number 5. TAVOLA QUINTA (Drawing 5).

Longitudinal Section Showing South Wall of Sanctuary, with Transept and Beginning of Nave.

Apparent from the treatment of the South Wall of the apse in this drawing is the fact that it belongs with *Catalogue Number 4*.

In the title inscriptions of the presentation drawings — as in this drawing — emphasis is placed on what Stampfle calls the "somewhat Borrominesque flavor of the decoration" (*An Unknown Group of Drawings*, p. 126). Piranesi was adamant about "le respect que l'on doit aux oeuvres des grands artistes" (Focillon I, p. 104). All his proposals for a new sanctuary for the Lateran reveal an extraordinary artistic harmony with Borromini's Baroque nave. Nor did he tire of pointing this out.

Pen and gray ink, with some heightening in brown ink in Piranesi's hand — the railing in the apse and the papal arms at the bottom are the most important instances. Ruled border in brown ink.

INSCRIBED: (in brown ink, lower right) *Cav. G. B. Piranesi fece.*

WATERMARK: No watermark and the paper is stronger than that of many drawings in the series.

H. 21¾″ (553 mm.) W. 34¹/₁₆″ (865 mm.)

CONDITION: On the back of the sheet the top edge has been reinforced, and there are four sealing wax stains, three across the bottom and one in the center. Some smudging across bottom of ruled border.

TOP: *Sezione ortografica di fianco della Tribuna, del Presbiterio, e dell'Esedra della Basilica Lateranense, immaginati con architettura corrispondente a [q]uella della gran Nave.*

BOTTOM: A wooden ruler marked off in *Palmi Romani* and at center the papal arms.

Catalogue Number 6. TAVOLA SESTA (Drawing 6).

Plan of Sanctuary with Screen of Columns and Ambulatory

The plan in this drawing presents a more elaborate proposal than the two already discussed in *Catalogue Numbers 1 and 4*, with a screen of columns separating the ambulatory from the presbytery; it is repeated, with but one minor change, in *Catalogue Number 7*, where a cross section is also presented. (For both drawings, see the legend on *Catalogue Number 11*..) Belonging to the same project are *Catalogue Numbers 8, 9, and 10*.

Fischer's reconstruction of the plan of Piranesi's "drittes Chorprojekt" (figure 13 and pp. 217ff.) is extremely close to ours. Significantly, it is based on the Pierpont Morgan Library drawing Number 55 which, however, is almost five feet across (see Stampfle, *An Unknown Group of Drawings*, p. 126;

Fischer, Figures 11 and 12). The over-sized format of Number 55 suggests that the four Morgan drawings for the Lateran (Numbers 55–58) seem never to have been part of the formal presentation group given to Cardinal Rezzonico in 1767. For the latter were apparently assembled on short notice and chosen on the basis of format — with the Morgan drawings either too small or too large to fit. *Catalogue Numbers 18, 19, and 23*, on the other hand, were carefully mounted to adjust them to the series.

The following implication seems unavoidable: Piranesi's proposals were completed before 1767. By that time — two years before Clement XIII's death — the project had become academic. Not a person to lose what advantages he still possessed with his patrons, Piranesi had a set of drawings prepared for presentation to Cardinal Rezzonico. Circumstantial support for this hypothesis is supplied by the use of his title, *Cavaliere del Sperone d'Oro*, which Pope Clement XIII bestowed on him, October 1766—and which would have helped to assuage the artist's pride.

Pen and gray ink, with brown ink in the magnificent vignette by Piranesi's hand. Ruled border, interrupted at each side by vignette, in brown ink.

INSCRIBED: (in brown ink, lower right) *Cav.ᴿ G. B. Piranesi fece.*

WATERMARK: ℙ

H. 35⁵/₁₆″ (896 mm.) W. 22⅛″ (562 mm.)

CONDITION: A tear on the right edge has been patched on the back, and there are five sealing wax stains. Otherwise in fairly good condition.

TOP: *Pianta della Tribuna, del Presbiterio, e dell'Esedra della Basilica Lateranense immaginati con architettura a seconda di quella della gran Nave.*

BOTTOM: A stone plaque placed before a large banderole, with palm branches, garlands, a cross, and a scale in Roman feet. On the small tablet above the plaque: PIUS CLE/MENS. Below, a medallion of Pope Clement with the inscription *Santa sui an VI. Clemens XIII.* On the plaque, the legend for the sanctuary plan, above: *1. Tribuna. 2. Presbiterio. 3. Esedra architettata, come gran Nave. 4. Colonnato, o steccato, che separa il Presbiterio della Tribuna. 5. Coro de' Musici. 6. Scala per salire al coro de' Musici. 7. Scala per salire ai Conditorj delle Reliquie. 8. Atrj architettati, come le Navi inferiori. 9. Ambulacro fra il Presbiterio, e la Tribuna, architettato, come le gran Nave. 10. Porta deretana della Basilica. 11. Porta della Sagrestia. 12. Coro d'inverno de'Canonici. 13. Cappella del Presepio. 14. Ingrandimento di essa, quanto il coro d'inverno. 15. Conditorio della Mensa di Nostro Signor Gesù Cristo. 16. Altar Papale. 17. Recinto e gradi per discendere al Conditorio delle sacre Teste de' SS. Apostoli Pietro e Paolo.*

Catalogue Number 7. TAVOLA SETTIMA (Drawing 7).

Plan and View of Sanctuary from the Transept

Through the sanctuary arch can be seen the semi-circular screen of paired columns, climaxed on the central axis by a representation of Christ in an elaborate oval frame. Beyond the screen, the upper wall of the apse is visible — suggestive of the emotion-engendering vistas of Palladio's Il Rendentore in Venice. As Wittkower has pointed out in his article on Piranesi's restoration of Sta. Maria del Priorato in Rome of 1764–1765 (*Piranesi*, pp. 99ff.), the artist retained his Venetian predilections in architecture: "He has primarily the subjective optical experience of the beholder in mind" (p. 107).

Pen and gray ink, with brown ink in Piranesi's hand within the sanctuary arch of the elevation. Plan in gray ink, with brown ink added sparingly for the steps, and to outline some of the piers. Brown ink also used to give the illusionistic effect of a separate sheet of paper which is curled in center, and for the ✹ monogram with garlands and tasselled rope. Ruled border in brown ink.

INSCRIBED: (in brown ink, lower right) *Cav.ᴿ G. B. Piranesi fece.*

WATERMARK: ℙ

H. 34⅞″ (887 mm.) W. 22⁵/₁₆″ (566 mm.)

CONDITION: The top, bottom, and left edges have later reinforcements on the back. Also on the back, sealing wax stains in upper right and in center (above the ✹ on the front). Ruled border smudged by water stains.

TOP: *Elevazione ortografica di fronte del Presbiterio della Basilica Lateranense notato nella sottoposta Pianta, ed accennato nella Tavola Sesta col numero 4.*

BOTTOM: *Pianta della Tribuna, del Presbiterio, e dell'Esedra della Basilica Lateranense.* With the note: *Le indicazioni della parti ommesse nella presente Pianta possono vedersi nella Tavola VI.* Scale marked off in Roman feet.

Catalogue Number 8. TAVOLA OTTAVA (Drawing 8).

Longitudinal Section Showing South Wall of Sanctuary, with Transept and Beginning of Nave.

As in the case of the preceding entry, this section belongs with *Catalogue Number 6*. It is close to the Pierpont Morgan Library drawing Number 55, but with certain changes. The forechoir just to the west of the crossing is a full bay, and this has caused changes in the vaulting. The paired pilasters that begin the columnar screen are absent from the Morgan drawing, and in place of the medallion of Christ on the screen, Number 55 climaxes the screen with a ball embellished by three figures.

The most important aspect of this project, also present in the Morgan drawing, is Piranesi's proposal to raise the roof of the sanctuary in two stages: the vaulting of the forechoir is raised above the roof of the nave and transept, and the half-dome is yet higher — allowing the half-dome to be lit by clerestory windows not visible from the crossing. Such special lighting would have lent to the freestanding colonnade in the apse a marvelously picturesque quality. But as Krautheimer has indicated, the construction of this immense structure would have been technically very difficult, to say the least, because of the terrain (see Stampfle, *An Unknown Group of Drawings*, p. 126 and n. 12).

Pen and gray ink over pencil guide lines; gray wash. Some brown ink in colonnade of chancel, etc. Ruled border in brown ink.

INSCRIBED: (in brown ink, legible although badly abraded, lower right) *Cav.ᴿ G. B. Piranesi fece.*

WATERMARK: ℞

H. 23⅛″ (587 mm.) W. 35⁵/₁₆″ (898 mm.)

CONDITION: Water stains, later patching on back, abraded in places. Nine stains from sealing wax on back. Ruled border smudged from water stains.

TOP: Wreath, ribbons and flowers and the scale in Roman feet, and on a large banderole: *Sezione ortografica di fianco della Tribuna, del Presbiterio, e dell'Esedra della Basilica Lateranense immaginati con architettura corrispondente a quella della gran Nave.*

Catalogue Number 9. TAVOLA NONA (Drawing 9).

Cross Section Showing Rear of Apse Facing West

This view of the apse shows, in the center, the door numbered 10 in *Catalogue Number 6*. However, the letters ABC are found in *Catalogue Number 11* rather than in the drawings cited in the inscription; they indicate a cross section taken through numbers 11, 9, and 15 of *Catalogue Number 6*.

The decoration of the vault in this drawing is the same as in *Catalogue Number 8* and close to the Morgan Library drawing Number 55: the alternation of panels of ornament with stars and cartouches in one and ovals and cartouches in the other. But the central panel in this drawing is unique. At the bottom, a flamboyant eagle, with wings spread, perches on an oval coffer of garlands. Above, oval and octagonal coffers overlap each other, with rosettes and shells. This central panel was given a detailed rendition by Piranesi in *Catalogue Number 18*, one of the most beautiful drawings of the series.

Pen, gray and brown ink, with washes. Ruled border in brown ink, with abrasion on left. Brown ink used to give the effect of a separate sheet of paper within the border, which has garlands at the top and curls into a roll at the bottom, with the papal arms and tasselled rope at the center of the paper roll — which has been cut for their insertion. Scale marked off in Roman feet.

INSCRIBED: (in brown ink, somewhat abraded, lower right) *Cav. G. B. Piranesi fece.*

WATERMARK: ℞

H. 34¹¹/₁₆″ (881 mm.) W. 22¹/₁₆″ (562 mm.)

CONDITION: Horizontal fold through center has weakened the paper. Badly abraded, considerable mold. On the back, left edge has later reinforcement and there are sealing wax stains.

TOP: *Elevazione della Tribuna della Basilica Lateranense notata in Pianta nelle Tavole VI. e VII. con le lett.* ABC [not on either drawing], *ed immaginata con architettura corrispondente a quella della gran Nave.* Followed by the legend: *1. Porta della Sagrestia. 2. Porta deretana della Basilica. 3. Conditorio della Mensa di Nostro Signor Gesù Cristo.*

Catalogue Number 10. TAVOLA DECIMA (Drawing 10).

Elevation Looking East, Showing the Colonnade Separating the Ambulatory from the Presbytery

The drawing exhibits exquisite precision, an incredible patience in its details, and a consummate pictorial quality in the variations of its washes. A *tour de force* of Piranesi's skilled draftsmanship, it adds weight to Focillon's remark, made in 1918: "Il n'est pas douteux qu'il l'exécutait [i.e., a calculated preparation for his copper plates] au compas et à la règle avec une précision absolue d'après les documents et les esquisses qu'il avait reúnis" (Focillon, I, p. 198). Indeed, Piranesi may have hoped at one time to etch his Lateran projects. But Focillon's remark reminds us that few of the many detail sketches that must have been made for the large finished drawings have so far turned up (see Stampfle, *An Unknown Group of Drawings*, Numbers 57 and 58; Fischer, figures 6, 7, 8a and b, 9a and b).

The reference in the inscription to number 4 on *Catalogue Number 6* (see below the Italian transcription of the note in this catalogue entry) correctly identifies the plan of the foreground element in the drawing, part of the bold concept embodied in the project under discussion (*Catalogue Numbers 6–10*). The double colonnade of the screen, open at the sides, is closed off in the center by a wall with three niches, topped by a pediment with a distinctive decoration which is handled in an austerely symmetrical, yet extraordinarily rich, manner. The same pediment design occurs in *Catalogue Number 23*, which is a detailed rendition of this central walled section of the screen with an alternate version of the attic to the left. The climax of this pedimented wall is a sculptural melange composed of a shell with garlands and volutes, above which are angels with their wings crossed in Borrominesque fashion. On the reverse, or eastern, side is the medallioned portrait of Christ, seen in *Catalogue Number 7*.

The arch seen behind this columnar structure — and in this view partially hidden by it — marks the division between transept and sanctuary (see *Catalogue Number 8*). Above, in a tympanum created by the abutment of the higher barrel vault — over the forechoir — with the transept roof, are the papal arms of Clement XIII against a decorative representation of a half-dome, the whole surrounded by a border of garlands.

The beautiful double-banded arch over the whole design is in a plane forward of the tympanum, at the juncture between the forechoir and the presbytery where the roof of the half-dome is raised above the barrel vault — allowing Piranesi the luxury of three circular clerestory windows. This arrangement is accurately depicted from the exterior in *Catalogue Number 12*. Two circular designs below the roof-line make a pattern of five circles within the double bands of the arch. They are interlocked by octagonal coffers. The rhythmic articulation of this composition is strongly reminiscent of Bramante's choir of Sta. Maria della Grazie in Milan (1492). This is another instance (see *Catalogue Number 7*) of the fact that "north-Italian parallels can easily be multiplied" (Wittkower, *Piranesi*, p. 108) not only in Piranesi's restoration of Sta. Maria del Priorato, but in his contemporary projects for the Lateran as well.

Pen and gray ink over ruled pencil guide lines. Brown ink in colonnade, and in powerfully rendered cartouches, garlands, and coffering. Ruled border in brown ink, and in illusionistic portrayal of separate sheet of paper, curled both top and bottom. Sheet held in place by a garland at the top. Below, vignette in brown ink composed of eagle's wings, serpent, pencil, compass, and ribbons. Scale in Roman feet. Loose parallel hatching setting off the sheet, in brown ink. The entire drawing in Piranesi's hand.

INSCRIBED: (in brown ink, lower right). *Cav.^R G. B. Piranesi fece.*

WATERMARK: ℞

H. 34½″ (876 mm.) W. 22⅜″ (564 mm.)

CONDITION: Some abrasion and water stains. Remains of sealing wax on back.

TOP: *Aspetto del di dietro del Recinto del Presbiterio della Basilica Lateranense delineato in Pianta nella Tavola VI. e. notatovi col numero 4.*

ON THE BANDEROLE: CLEMENS XIII PONTIS. MAX. PONTIFICAT. . . SUI ANNO. VI.

Catalogue Number 11. TAVOLA UNDECIMA (Drawing 11).

Plan of Sanctuary with Screen of Columns and Ambulatory

This plan represents a variation on the plan in *Catalogue Number 6*, thus belonging with the elaborate project of *Catalogue Numbers 6–10*. There are two major differences: the papal altar and baldacchino have been moved from the crossing to the first bay of the sanctuary (see *Catalogue Number 12*), and an aisle has been provided (G) to give clerics easier access to the presbytery on ceremonial occasions. Of the seven plans in the series, only *Catalogue Numbers 11 and 16* show the papal altar in this position.

There is a particularly interesting historical issue involved. The Lateran was an imperial foundation, begun under Constantine ca. 313. The high and wide transept is a medieval structure. Krautheimer describes the fourth century arrangement: "The western section of the nave directly in front of the apse [in functional terms, the nave belonged rather to the people than to their bishop and his clerics] . . . would shelter the altar; the apse held seats for bishop and clergy [Piranesi's *Presbiterio*]. Across its opening extended a huge fastigium of silver, apparently supported by a double row of columns" (see Stampfle, *An Unknown Group of Drawings*, p. 26). Silver statues below presented Christ the Teacher to the congregation, but the clergy in the apse were presented with the image of the Resurrected Christ. As Krautheimer says, "Christ revealed himself in different but complementary aspects to the people and, as it were, to the high officials of his court."

At the time of Borromini's remodelling of the nave (1646–1649), the high altar was in the transept, in the same position as Piranesi uses in five of the seven plans (see Fischer, figure 2 for Rasponi's plan of 1656). That is, the high altar was in a position equivalent to the original arrangement — the transept having

added, simply, much needed space to the nave. But in this plan Piranesi indicates (E) that the papal altar has been moved to the first bay west of the transept — *the Esedra* — *dare alla gran Nave e alla Crociata un più ampio e libero spazio.* Piranesi was not thus breaking with the early building tradition of the Church. For this plan more than any other in the series gives expression to the hierarchical and ceremonial functions of the Pope's Seat as Bishop of Rome, and to the holy relics of Peter and Paul which it houses. The fact that when a new sanctuary was finally built (1876–1887) under Leo XIII an *Esedra* or forechoir was inserted, gives credence to the idea that ceremonial grandeur was still a much desired effect over a century later.

Pen and gray ink, with gray wash which, in nave piers, fades off. Brown ink in some lines in sanctuary, and dotted lines for nave plan. Ruled border in brown ink.

INSCRIBED: (in brown ink, lower right) *Cav. G. B. Piranesi fece.*

WATERMARK: ℞

H. 35¹/₆″ (890 mm.) W. 22⅛″ (562 mm.)

CONDITION: The bottom right corner has been repaired with an extra sheet on the back. Horizontal fold through the center, and sealing wax in center of the back of the sheet, have weakened the paper. Badly abraded in parts. Brown ink has eaten through the paper, left and right of one border.

TOP: *Pianta della Tribuna, del Presbiterio e dell'Esedra della Basilica Lateranense immaginati con architettura corrispondente alla gran Nave, e a' Laterali della medesima.*

BOTTOM: *Scala di Palmi Romani.* Just above the scale, the following legend: *Spiegazione delle note. A. Gran Tribuna con la cui ampiezza si e inteso di dare alla Basilica una testa corrispondente alla sua vastità, e fare un corpo di Chiesa proporzionato in ogni parte, come dimostra il disegno aggiunto di tutta la Basilica. B. Altare del Presbiterio distaccato dalla Tribuna, e con due ale di colonne situate sopra une precinzione che racchiude gli stalli de' Canonici. C. Ambulacro fra la Tribuna e l'Presbiterio che da l'ingresso libero a chi entra per la gran porta deretana segnata col numero 1, ed a chi viene per la porta della Sagrestia accenata col numero 2. D. Cappella dietro l'altare del Presbiterio riservato o per un magnifico mausoleo, o per dedicarei a qualche Santo. E. Esedra ove si è stimato di trasferiere l'Altare Papale per approssimarlo al Presbiterio cosi arretato, e dare alle gran Nave e alla Crociate un più ampio e libero spazio. F. Recinto de gradi per discendere al Conditorio delle sacre Teste de' SS. Apostili Pietro e Paolo, Situato sotto l'Altare Papale. G. Spazi che separano il Presbiterio dall'Esedra, per dare l'ingresso al Clero, allor che viene per salire ai cori dei Musici. K. Conditori della Mensa di Nostro Signor Gesù Cristo. L. Gran Nave della Basilica, la cui architettura adornata di nicchi e pilastri ricorre intorno all Crociata, all'Esedra, ed alla gran Tribuna, secondo che accennano i numeri dal 3 fino 12. M. Architettura delle navi inferiori, con ciu son adornati gli anditi già accennati con la nota H. N. Capella del coro invernale de' Canonici.*

Catalogue Number 12. TAVOLA DUODECIMA (Drawing 12).

Cross Section Showing Projected West Wall of Transept, with Baldacchino Placed Inside Sanctuary Arch

This drawing is almost entirely by the hand of a draftsman — the sole exception is the baldacchino. The description of Piranesi's workshop in the late eighteenth century biography by

Legrand is relevant here. Speaking of the artist's *cruelle idée* that at his death his life's work, including his copper plates, would be scattered and go for naught, Legrand wrote: "Il . . . craignait toujours que le jeunesse de son fils ne fût un obstacle à ce qu'il continuât de maintenir l'ordre établi dans ses ateliers où plusieurs dessinateurs et graveurs travaillaient sous sa direction immédiate, et remplissaient chacun la tache qu'il leur assignait en particulier, mais il se reservait toujours les parties difficiles et l'accord général" (p. 72).

The cross section of the transept cuts through the double staircase leading down to the crypt; the papal altar is in the first bay of the sanctuary, as in *Catalogue Number 11*. This is the only cross section of the transept showing the intention to remodel its western wall in a Borrominesque fashion, in contrast to *Catalogue Numbers 2, 4, and 7* which simply record the existing wall.

The inscription on *Catalogue Number 14* connects it with this drawing, as well as *Catalogue Number 13* and the missing Drawing Number 13 (presumably also a section). There are certain problems, however. For while both *Catalogue Numbers 12 and 14* have an altar painting at the head of the apse of which *Catalogue Number 14* is a cross section, this drawing shows a columnar screen to either side of it. *Catalogue Number 14* has a different arrangement (see *Catalogue Number 13*). On the other hand, the clerestory windows of the sanctuary connect the drawing with the elaborate project of *Catalogue Numbers 6–11*; there is no clerestory in *Catalogue Number 14*. Clearly, then, this drawing is intermediate and the inscription referring to it is inaccurate.

Pen and gray ink over pencil guide lines. Brown ink in the baldacchino, in Piranesi's hand, and in cartouche with papal arms at top of the chancel arch. Ruled border in brown ink, interrupted along top by triangular clerestory of sanctuary rising above the transept roof.

INSCRIBED: (in brown ink, lower right) *Cav.^R G. B. Piranesi fece.*

WATERMARK: ℙ

H. 22⅜" (567 mm.) W. 34⅞" (885 mm.)

CONDITION: Abrasion in baldacchino and cartouche areas. Five stains on back from sealing wax.

ON LARGE BANDEROLE ABOVE CHANCEL ARCH: CLEMENS XIII. PO[NT MA]X A VI.

BOTTOM: Scale marked in *Palmi Romani.*

Catalogue Number 13. TAVOLA DECIMAQUARTA (Drawing 14).*

Plan of Sanctuary with Ambulatory

The solution presented in this plan, which belongs with *Catalogue Numbers 14 and 15*, is seen in a more grandiloquent

*Drawing 13 is missing.

version in *Catalogue Numbers 16 and 17*. The robust columns — in single file — of the screen separating the "tribune-presbytery" are seen from within the central space as being on a high pedestal — the choir (5) is raised above its level. The result is to lend a tone of solemn Neo-classical majesty to the apse as symbol of the Seat of Authority of the Bishop of Rome.

Pen and gray ink, with some lines in brown ink. Ruled border in brown ink.

INSCRIBED: (in brown ink, lower right of legend) *Cav. G. B. Piranesi fece.*

WATERMARK: ℙ

H. 34¹¹/₁₆" (882 mm.) W. 22³/₁₆" (563 mm.)

CONDITION: Mold. Sealing wax stains on back at corners and in center.

TOP: *Pianta della Tribuna, del Presbiterio, e dell'Esedra della Basilica Lateranense, immaginati con architettura corrispondente a quella della gran Nave.*

BOTTOM: Scale marked off in *Palmi Romani.* Below the scale, within a ruled frame, the following legend: *1. Tribuna e Presbiterio. 2. Esedra ove ricorre l'architettura della gran Nave. 3. Altar Papale. 4. Scale per discendere al Conditorio della SS. Teste de' SS. Pietro e Paolo. 5. Cori de' Musici. 6. Scale per salire ai Conditori delle Reliquie. 7. Altri sottoposti ai Conditori delle Reliquie, e architettati come le navi inferiori. 8. Porta deretana della Tribuna, donde entrare nel Presbiterio. 9. Porte deretane della Basilica. 10. Andito che mette nella Sagrestia. 11. Coro da inverno de Canonici. 12. Cappella del Presepio. 13. La medesima Cappella quanto la corrispondente del Coro da inverno de' Canonici.*

Catalogue Number 14. TAVOLA DECIMAQUINTA (Drawing 15).

Cross Section Through the Choir, Corresponding to Drawing 14

This section cuts through the apse at numbers 5, 1, 5 of the plan (*Catalogue Number 13*), which shows the bases of the elaborate candelabra flanking the altar. *Catalogue Number 15* provides a longitudinal section of this project (see also *Catalogue Number 12*).

An exceedingly picturesque drawing, Piranesi's control of tonal effects is here illustrated not only through the variety of washes he uses — in the rolled edges of the paper, for instance, of the oblique ray of light that falls on the altar painting — but also in the precise inking of the architectural decoration. Whether an icon of Christ, or, in a pediment, the Lamb of God placed upon God's Word, the Bible, or the coffers in a half-dome being rhythmically interwoven by garlands, lavish attention has been given to the ornamentation. In the center of the apse, the peculiar juxtaposition of shapes again calls northern Italy to mind — the painting in an arched frame; above, a triangular pediment cornice with volutes; then the rectangular panel which interrupts the frieze, above which is a large pediment; finally the garland ropes of the vault. The family resemblance this time is to the decorative tradition of Piedmont: Guarini and Juvarra.

Pen and brown ink, with gray and brown washes. Ruled border, in brown ink, interrupted on both sides by rolled edges of separate sheet of paper in loose brown washes. Sheet held in place by ribbons and garlands at the top, with another, narrower, sheet projecting above with the title. Below, vignette in brown ink composed of an open book with pen, a serpent, ribbons and garlands; the vignette overlaps a *Scala di Palmi Romani*. Loose parallel hatching to either side of sheet in brown ink. The drawing in Piranesi's hand.

INSCRIBED: (in brown ink, toward lower right) *Cav. G. B. Piranesi f.*

WATERMARK: ℟

H. 35⁵/₁₆″ (897 mm.) W. 22½″ (572 mm.)

CONDITION: The acid ink has eaten through the paper in several places and, in one case, has burned out the paper. On the back there are later reinforcements along the bottom and right edges, and five sealing wax stains.

TOP: *Elevazione ortografica della Tribuna, e del Presbiterio della Basilica Lateranense corrispondente alle Pianta, ed alla Sezione, delineate nella Tavole XII. XIII. XIV.*

Catalogue Number 15. TAVOLA DECIMASESTA (Drawing 16).

Longitudinal Section Showing South Wall of Sanctuary, with Transept and Beginning of Nave

Belonging with *Catalogue Numbers 13 and 14*, this drawing illustrates the almost imperial grandeur of the project. The walls of the choir stall are decorated with bold ornaments, and in each intercolumniation an eagle perches on top of the choir stall. The monumental composite columns rise to a continuous architrave and frieze — the latter with oval panels linked by garland borders, containing the cross as well as the tower from the Rezzonico arms. The ornamentation of the vault includes tremendous star-and-circle coffers. *Catalogue Number 17* provides an alternative version, with the forechoir greatly enlarged.

Pen, gray and brown ink, with rich tonalities of gray and brown washes. Ruled border in brown ink. Piranesi's hand in the right (sanctuary) section and in heightening with brown ink of details in the nave.

INSCRIBED: (in brown ink, lower right) *Cav.ᴿ G. B. Piranesi fece.*

WATERMARK: None.

H. 21⅞″ (556 mm.) W. 35⅛″ (893 mm.)

CONDITION: There are water stains which have caused the ink to run, especially along the lower border. On the back, the paper has a later reinforcement along the top edge, and there are traces of sealing wax. The border ink has eaten through the paper in many places.

TOP: *Sezione ortografica di fianco della Tribuna, del Presbiterio, e dell'Esedra della Basilica Lateranense immaginati con architettura corrispondente a quella della gran Nave, e de' lati.* Just below, a scale marked off in *Palmi Romani*.

BOTTOM: *1. Uno de' Coretti da mostrar le Sacre Reliquie. 2. Coro de' Musici della Cappella.*

Catalogue Number 16. TAVOLA DECIMASETTIMA (Drawing 17).

Plan of Sanctuary

The plan is related to *Catalogue Number 13*, but there are important differences. The papal altar and baldacchino have been placed inside the sanctuary arch (see *Catalogue Number 11*), and the forechoir has been enlarged by two bays (see *Catalogue Number 17*) so that the choir to either side is moved eastward. In the apse, the large columns have been placed against the wall on a continuous pedestal, above which are niches in the intercolumniation.

Pen and gray ink over pencil guide lines. At the bottom, a gray wash cuts obliquely across the plaque, with the legend in brown ink. Below the plaque, a scale marked off in *Palmi Romani*. At its center a vignette with lion's head within the cartouche, and palm branches and garlands. The ornamental vignette, in Piranesi's hand, in brown ink. Ruled border in brown ink.

INSCRIBED: (in brown ink, lower right of the plaque) *Cav. G. B. Piranesi f.*

WATERMARK: ℟

H. 35¹/₆″ (891 mm.) W. 22¼″ (565 mm.)

CONDITION: There are stains from sealing wax on the back, and considerable mold.

BELOW PLAN OF THE SANCTUARY: *Pianta della Tribuna, del Presbiterio, e dell'Esedra della Basilica Lateranense immaginati con architettura corrispondente a quella della gran Nave.*

ON THE PLAQUE, THE FOLLOWING LEGEND: *1. Tribuna, e Presbiterio. 2. Esedra, Ove ricorre l'architettura della gran Nave. 3. Altar Papale trasferito all'ingresso dell'Esedra. 4. Cori de' Musici. 5. Spogliatoj de' Musici. 6. Scale per salire ai Conditori delle Reliquie. 7. Atri architettati come le navi inferiori. 8. Porte deretane della Basilica. 9. Andito che mette nella Sagrestia. 10. Coro da inverno de' Canonici. 11. Cappella del Presepio. 12. La medesima ingrandita quanto la corrispondente del Coro da inverno.*

Catalogue Number 17. TAVOLA DECIMAOTTAVA (Drawing 18).

Longitudinal Section Showing North Wall of Sanctuary, with Transept and Beginning of Nave

This is the only longitudinal section in the series to show the existing north wall of the transept and nave. It belongs with the plan, *Catalogue Number 16*, representing a project that is greatly expanded. Indeed, this sanctuary, if built, would be enormous: according to the scale given on the drawing, the sanctuary structure is one hundred sixty-seven Roman feet in length. By comparison, the project discussed in *Catalogue Numbers 13 and 14* certainly would provide a sanctuary of impressive dimensions, one hundred twenty Roman feet in length according to the scale given in *Catalogue Number 15* — yet this project is longer by one third. The treatment of the forechoir in this version supports the point already made (see *Catalogue Number 5*), that Piranesi was serious in his desire to harmonize his sanctuary with the Baroque style of Borromini's nave. By making the forechoir three bays instead of one, he was able to recreate — as nowhere else — the alternating rhythm of Borromini's nave — narrow sculptural niche, wide arched opening, narrow sculptural niche.

Both this project and the preceding version (*Catalogue Numbers 13–15*) show that Piranesi has abandoned the idea of providing clerestory windows to light the sanctuary.

Pen, gray and brown ink, with rich tonalities of gray and brown washes. Ruled border in brown ink. Piranesi's hand in the left (sanctuary) section.

INSCRIBED: (in brown ink, lower right) *Cav.ᴿ G. B. Piranesi f.*

WATERMARK: None and the paper of the same composition as *Catalogue Number 15*.

H. 22⅞″ (582 mm.) W. 35¹¹/₁₆″ (906 mm.)

CONDITION: Abrasion, and the paper is cracked on left. On the back, there is a later reinforcement along the top edge and sealing wax stains.

TOP: *Sezione ortografica di fianco della Tribuna del Presbiterio e dell'Esedra della Basilica Lateranense immaginati con architettura corrispondente a quella della gran Nave.* Just below a scale marked off in *Palmi Romani.*

WITHIN THE ARCH OF THE SANCTUARY DOOR TO THE CHOIR, A MEDALLION OF CLEMENT XIII AND THE INSCRIPTION: CLEMENS XIII PONTIFEX MAXIMUS ANN. VI. [1764]

BOTTOM: *1 . 2 . Coretti per mostrar le Sacre Reliquie, che si conservano nella Basilica. 3. Coro de' Musici della Capella.*

Catalogue Number 18. TAVOLA DECIMANONA (Drawing 19).

Panel of Vaulting Coffers, Corresponding to Drawing 9

This magnificent drawing, an enlargement of the central panel of the vault in *Catalogue Number 9*, is one of two such enlargements in the series — the other is *Catalogue Number 23*, which is an enlargement of *Catalogue Number 10*. Together with *Catalogue Number 19* — like them, a drawing on the paper used by the artist for his etchings, by his hand, and adjusted to the format of the presentation series — they support the hypothesis (see *Catalogue Number 6*) that the projects of the presentation series date from before 1767, that drawings which had similar format were then provided with title inscriptions, the inscribed signature of the artist — with his new title — and ruled borders, all in brown ink.

Pen and brown ink over pencil, with brown washes. Ruled border in brown ink, with

additional ruled border on both sides of pasted sheet also in brown ink. The drawing is entirely in Piranesi's hand.

INSCRIBED: (in brown ink, lower right of the backing sheet) *Cav.ᴿ G. B. Piranesi fece.*

WATERMARKS: Indecipherable, on backing sheet.

H. (to ruled borders) 33¹⁵/₁₆″ (862 mm.) W. 21³/₁₆″ (537 mm.)
H. (mounted sheet) 30¹³/₁₆″ (782 mm.) W. 12³/₁₆″ (310 mm.)

CONDITION: In relatively good condition, although spotted.

BOTTOM: *Dimostrazione in grande de' Lavori delineati ne' compartimenti della gran Tribuna che si mostra alla Tavola Nona.*

Catalogue Number 19. TAVOLA VIGESIMA (Drawing 20).

Papal Altar and Baldacchino

The drawing exhibits Piranesi's polemical advocacy, in his *Osservazioni . . . Parere sul architettura* (1764), described under *Catalogue Number 43*, of profuse ornamentation in architecture — the series of banded fields of decoration on the column shafts, the band of fretwork running across the pedestals of altar and columns, the garlands and volutes covering the repository over the altar for the relics of Peter and Paul. It can be compared with the earlier drawing in Bologna of a Portico Before Terraced Palace [sic](Thomas, Number 43; ca. 1758–1763), which has the banded columnar reliefs, and the same running fretwork. But the ornament is not as concentrated or involved as in this drawing.

According to Rohault de Fleury (pp. 224–25), the discovery of the heads of Peter and Paul — each complete even to the teeth and enclosed in a silver vase was made by Pope Urban V on March 1, 1368. The Pope immediately ordered gold reliquary busts for the relics, which are shown in *Catalogue Numbers 21 and 22*.

Pen and brown ink over pencil guide lines, brown and gray washes. Ruled border in brown ink. The drawing is entirely in Piranesi's hand.

INSCRIBED: (in brown ink, lower right of the backing sheet) *Cav. G. B. Piranesi fece.*

WATERMARK ON MOUNTED SHEET: Fleur-de-lis in double circle with CB above; on the backing sheet VIT.

H. (to ruled borders) 33¹³/₁₆″ (859 mm.) W. 20¼″ (539 mm.)
H. (mounted sheet) 29³/₁₆″ (741 mm.) W. 18¹¹/₁₆″ (474 mm.)

CONDITION: Mold on both sheets and some abrasion—e.g., on the left hand column. Sealing wax stains on the back.

BOTTOM: *Altro progetto dell' Altar Papale della Basilica Lateranense veduto dalla parte della gran nave della stessa Basilica adornato con un' urna da riporvi le Sacre Teste de' Santi Apostoli Pietro e Paolo.*

Catalogue Number 20. TAVOLA VIGESIMAPRIMA (Drawing 21).

Plan and Elevation of Papal Altar and Baldacchino

The inscription of Piranesi's name on this drawing — and on the baldacchino designs of *Catalogue Numbers 21 and 22* — differs from that of all other drawings in the series. These three are by the same hand, an assistant in the *atelier*: although the designs employ motifs found in the Lateran proposals, their ornamentation is handled in a dry and rather academic manner, with studiously fussy ornamentation.

Pen and gray ink over pencil, with gray washes. Delicate emphasis in brown ink. Ruled border in brown ink. The drawing is undoubtedly by an assistant to Piranesi.

INSCRIBED: (in brown ink, lower right) *Cav. G. Baťta Piranesi f[ece]*.

WATERMARK: ℞

H. 35¼″ (895 mm.) W. 23½″ (597 mm.)

CONDITION: In the candelabra flanking the baldacchino, ink has been scraped off and corrections have been made — also in ink. There is abrasion in the plan and the end of the right cornucopia. Stains from sealing wax on the back. Ink of border has eaten through the paper.

BELOW THE ELEVATION: *Uno de'progetti dell' Altar Papale, veduto dalla parte della mensa che riguarda La Tribuna, ed inventato sul gusto del Boromino, secondo il quale è stata rinnovata la Basilica.*

Catalogue Number 21. TAVOLA VIGESIMA-SECONDA (Drawing 22).

Papal Altar and Baldacchino, Flanked by Elaborate Candelabra

Pen and brown ink over pencil, with gray and brown washes. There are pencil lines for squaring the drawing (see *Catalogue Number 22*). Ruled border in brown ink. The drawing is by the same draftsman as the one above. (*Catalogue Number 20*).

INSCRIBED: (in brown ink, lower right) *Cav. G. Baťta Piranesi fece.*

WATERMARK: ℞

H. 35⁵/₁₆″ (900 mm.) W. 23½″ (597 mm.)

CONDITION: There is considerable mold and spotting, and on the back there are stains from sealing wax.

Catalogue Number 22. TAVOLA VIGESIMATERZA (Drawing 23).

Papal Altar and Baldacchino, Flanked by Elaborate Candelabra

Pen and brown ink over pencil, with gray wash. Pencil lines for squaring the drawing, as in *Catalogue Number 21*. Ruled border in brown ink. The drawing is in the same hand as *Catalogue Numbers 20 and 21*.

INSCRIBED: (in brown ink, lower right) *Cav. G. Baťta Piranesi fece.*

WATERMARK: ℞

H. 35¹¹/₁₆″ (906 mm.) W. 23⅜″ (594 mm.)

CONDITION: There is a large water stain on the left, and a great deal of mold on the paper. On the back, sealing wax stains. Ruled border is smudged by water stain at bottom left.

BOTTOM: *Altro progetto dell'Altar Papale della Basilica Lateranense rappresentato e veduto dalla parte della mensa, che riguarda la Tribuna, e inventato su lo stile del Boromino, secondo il quale è stata rinnovata la Basilica.*

Catalogue Number 23. TAVOLA VIGESIMAQUINTA (Drawing 25).*

Design for Colonnade Separating the Ambulatory from the Presbytery (seen in Drawing 10) with Alternate Version of Attic to Left

This drawing in large format (see *Catalogue Number 18*) shows the central area in *Catalogue Number 10*, where the attic design follows the right-side alternative. In addition to having been mounted by 1767 (see also *Catalogue Numbers 18 and 19*), this drawing was folded down the right side to make it conform to the format of the other presentation drawings. The style is that of *Catalogue Number 19*, and the design close to that of the vignette at the end of Piranesi's text in his *Osservazioni . . . Parere sul architettura* (p. 16), which is signed Piranesi *inv. ed. inc.* This indicates that at least this drawing — and probably *Catalogue Number 19* as well — can be dated as early as 1764, when the *Parere* appeared.

Pen and brown ink over pencil, with brown and gray washes. Ruled border in brown ink. Although the only drawing of the series without Piranesi's name inscribed, it is unquestionably by his hand.

WATERMARK ON MOUNTED SHEET: Fleur-de-lis in double circle with CB above.

H. 36⅝″ (903 mm.) W. 28⁷/₁₆″ (723 mm.)

CONDITION: The fold down the side has contemporary reinforcement on the back. The sheet had also been folded through the center, and this fold has contemporary reinforcement as well. Mold in the center of the mounted sheet, and sealing wax stains are on the backing sheet.

*Drawing 24 is missing.

Catalogue Number 24a–n. THE CARCERI (The Prisons). State I.

Etched title:
INVENZIONI / CAPRIC DICARCERI / ALL ACQVA FORTE/ DATTE IN LVCE / DA GIOVANI / BVZARD IN / ROMA MER-CANT / AL CORSO

We do not know precisely when Piranesi etched his early masterpiece, the *Carceri*. It is probably safe to assign them to the later 1740's. The earliest impressions with a certain date are those included in the *Magnificenze di Roma* of 1751. This rare collection of miscellaneous works mentions in its lengthy title ". . . *molti capricci di carceri sotterranee.*" Hind describes three copies which do indeed contain first edition *Carceri* with title in second state.

The splendid Sackler set, exhibited here, may also come from a copy of the *Magnificenze*. Its plates were originally published folded into a smaller volume. The remains of guard stubs are still pasted along the fold of each plate. It is also possible that they come from an *Opere varie* set. Hind mentions one such copy in the Soane Museum (p. 82). Or, they could have appeared separately in a slender volume. Only plate [4] has a clearly legible watermark, a fleur-de-lis within a circle. This corresponds to Hind's watermark number 1, noted on the earliest impressions of the *Vedute di Roma*, including those in copies of the *Magnificenze di Roma*. It should also be remarked that the plates are trimmed to a uniform size and gilded on all four sides.

CONTENTS: Fourteen unnumbered plates including title.

NOTES: Later impressions have the title plate in a revised state: Buzard is corrected to read Bouchard as in the Sackler plate which is here described as State IA (see Catalogue entries below under *Catalogue Number 24a* and illustration). Hind's numbering of the states has been used for identification of Catalogue entries but in the case of the title plate illustrated as part of the Sackler State I set, Hind indicates it as State II, and since it is clearly different from the title page in the Sackler State II *Carceri*, Hind's designation is set aside for a "State IA" designation. Hind's titles have been used for the identification of the Catalogue entries as well. In the illustrations and the catalogue entries below, the first state of each plate in the series alternates with its revised or later state. The earlier state is listed *Catalogue Numbers 24a–n*, the later state is listed *Catalogue Numbers 25a–p*. Since there are two additional plates in State II, there is no meshing of letters in the numbering system except for 24a and 25a.

Catalogue Numbers 25a–p. THE CARCERI. State II (Second work in the volume of the *Opere varie*, Volume [I] Sackler set).

Etched title:
CARCERI / D'INVENZIONE / DI G. BATTISTA / PIRANESI / ARCHIT / VENE / Piranesi F.

Again the date is not certain. It is commonly assumed to be around 1761, the supposed date of Piranesi's move to the address given on Plate 2 (see NOTES below).

In this new edition, Piranesi added Plates 2 and 5* and reworked the original fourteen to startling effect. He solidified the structural forms, added strong shadows, and filled these once broadly-conceived fantasies with details. These range from large foreground elements which transform whole compositions, to tiny figures climbing distant staircases. These staircases (and other new vistas) add endless spacial complexities. In general, these changes bring the plates stylistically into line with Plates 2 and 5. These, in turn, are close in spirit to Piranesi's current archaeological visions such as the frontispieces to the *Antichità romane*.

It has become clear of late that a transitional stage with a number of intermediate states comes between the first and second states described by Hind. We know that during a certain period Piranesi actually offered a set of 15 *Carceri*.

The first known state of the *Catalogo* (ca. 1761) lists fifteen. The second known state (also ca. 1761) lists a completed set of sixteen. Piranesi must have spent a considerable period of time reworking the original fourteen plates. From time to time during this period, he would number individual plates. An impression of the series in one of these intermediate states is at Princeton University. It is described in the Colnaghi Piranesi catalogue, 1973/74 (Colnaghi, introduction to item 44) as partly reworked but with only one plate numbered (XVI). Colnaghi's item 44 itself is a comparable set. In it, plates VII and XVI have been numbered. In the Sackler copy, all have been numbered.

CONTENTS: New edition with sixteen numbered plates including title.

WATERMARKS: The legible watermarks are of Hind's type 3: a fleur-de-lis within a double circle with a monogram "CB" above.

IMPRESSIONS: The plates are printed in dark brown inks and show poorly printed or abraded patches.

NOTES: Imprint on plate 2: *Presso l' Autore a Strada Felice vicino alla Trinità de' Monti. Fogli sedici, al prezzo di paoli venti.* This set of impressions comes from Volume [1], *Opere varie* of the Sackler Piranesi set.

*These plates are listed below as *Catalogue Numbers 25b and 25e* and as State: Hind I since they were, at the time of the second state, new to the series.

Catalogue Number 24a. THE CARCERI.

Title Plate

UNSIGNED.

ETCHING: H. 21¼″ (540 mm.) W. 16³/₁₆″ (414 mm.)*

STATE: I A (Hind II)

F. 24. Hind 1.

Catalogue Number 25a. THE CARCERI.

Title Plate

SIGNED: below towards left: Piranesi F.

NUMBERED: I upper left.

STATE: II (Hind III).

F. 24. Hind 1.

Catalogue Number 25b. THE CARCERI.

An Architectural Medley, with a Man on the Rack in the Foreground.

SIGNED: lower right margin: Piranesi F.

NUMBERED: II upper right.

ETCHING: H. 22″ (559 mm.) W. 16⅜″ (416 mm.)

STATE: Hind I.

F. 25. Hind 2.

Catalogue Number 24b. THE CARCERI.

A Vaulted Building with a Staircase Leading round a Central Column with Barred Window in the Center.

UNSIGNED.

ETCHING: H. 21⁷/₁₆″ (545 mm.) W. 15⁵/₁₆″ (414 mm.)

STATE: Hind I.

F. 26. Hind 3.

Catalogue Number 25c. THE CARCERI.

A Vaulted Building with a Staircase Leading round a Central Column with a Barred Window in the Center.

SIGNED: lower left: Piranesi F.

NUMBERED: III upper left.

STATE: Hind II.

F. 26. Hind 3.

Catalogue Number 24c. THE CARCERI.

A Lofty Arch with Vista on to an Arcade Surmounted by a Frieze.

UNSIGNED.

ETCHING: H. 21⁷/₁₆″ (545 mm.) W. 16¼″ (413 mm.)

STATE: Hind I.

F. 27. Hind 4.

Catalogue Number 25d. THE CARCERI.

A Lofty Arch with Vista on to an Arcade Surmounted by a Frieze.

SIGNED: lower right: Piranesi F.

NUMBERED: IV upper right.

STATE: Hind II.

F. 27. Hind 4.

Catalogue Number 25e. THE CARCERI.

A Perspective of Roman Arches with Two Lions Carved in Relief on Stone Slabs in the Foreground.

SIGNED: lower right: Piranesi F.

NUMBERED: V upper left.

ETCHING: H. 21³¹/₃₂″ (558 mm.) W. 16⁷/₃₂″ (412 mm.)

STATE: Hind I.

F. 28. Hind 5.

*The measurements are taken from the first state. The second state impressions, from the same original plate, are of identical size.

Catalogue Number 24d. THE CARCERI.

A Perspective of Arches with a Smoking Fire in the Center.

UNSIGNED.

ETCHING: H. 21¼″ (540 mm.) W. 15¾″ (399 mm.)

STATE: Hind I.

F. 29. Hind 6.

Catalogue Number 24f. THE CARCERI.

A Vast Interior with Trophies at the Foot of a Broad Staircase and Two Large Flags on the Left.

UNSIGNED.

ETCHING: H. 21½″ (547 mm.) W. 15³/₁₆″ (401 mm.)

STATE: Hind I.

F. 31. Hind 8.

Catalogue Number 25f. THE CARCERI.

A Perspective of Arches with a Smoking Fire in the Center.

SIGNED: lower left: Piranesi F.

NUMBERED: VI upper right.

STATE: Hind II.

F. 29. Hind 6.

Catalogue Number 25h. THE CARCERI.

A Vast Interior with Trophies at the Foot of a Broad Staircase and Two Large Flags on the Left.

SIGNED: lower left: Piranesi F.

NUMBERED: VIII upper right.

STATE: Hind II.

F. 31. Hind 8.

Catalogue Number 24e. THE CARCERI.

An Immense Interior with Numerous Wooden Galleries and a Drawbridge in the Center.

SIGNED: lower left: Piranesi f.

ETCHING: H. 21½″ (547 mm.) W. 16¹/₁₆″ (408 mm.)

STATE: Hind I.

F. 30. Hind 7.

Catalogue Number 24g. THE CARCERI.

A Prison Door Surmounted by a Colossal Wheel-shaped Opening, Crossed by Beams.

SIGNED: lower left: Piranesi f.

ETCHING: H. 21¾″ (553 mm.) W. 16″ (406 mm.)

STATE: Hind I.

F. 32. Hind 9.

Catalogue Number 25g. THE CARCERI.

An Immense Interior with Numerous Wooden Galleries and a Drawbridge in the Center.

SIGNED: lower left: Piranesi f.

NUMBERED: VII upper left.

STATE: Hind II.

F. 30. Hind 7.

Catalogue Number 25i. THE CARCERI.

A Prison Door Surmounted by a Colossal Wheel-shaped Opening Crossed by Beams.

SIGNED: lower left: Piranesi f.

NUMBERED: IX upper left.

STATE: Hind II.

F. 32. Hind 9.

Catalogue Number 24h. THE CARCERI.

A Vast Gallery with Round Arches and a Group of Prisoners on a Projecting Stone in the Foreground.

SIGNED: lower left: Piranesi f.

ETCHING: H. 16¼″ (413 mm.) W. 21⁵/₁₆″ (542 mm.)

STATE: Hind I.

F. 33. Hind 10.

Catalogue Number 25j. THE CARCERI.

A Vast Gallery with Round Arches and a Group of Prisoners on a Projecting Stone in the Foreground.

SIGNED: lower left: Piranesi f.

NUMBERED: X upper right.

STATE: Hind II.

F. 33. Hind 10.

Catalogue Number 24i. THE CARCERI.

A Series of Galleries with Round Arches and a Cranelike Construction of Beams in the Right Foreground.

UNSIGNED.

ETCHING: H. 16¼″ (423 mm.) W. 21³/₁₆″ (554 mm.)

STATE: Hind I.

F. 34. Hind 11.

Catalogue Number 25k. THE CARCERI.

A Series of Galleries with Round Arches and a Cranelike Construction of Beams in the Right Foreground.

SIGNED: lower left: Piranesi F.

NUMBERED: XI above towards right.

STATE: Hind II.

F. 34. Hind 11.

Catalogue Number 24j. THE CARCERI.

An Arched Chamber with Lower Arches Surmounted by Posts and Chains. Strong Light Entering from the Right Hand.

SIGNED: lower left: Piranesi f.

ETCHING: H. 16¼″ (413 mm.) W. 21³/₁₆″ (554 mm.)

STATE: Hind I.

F. 35. Hind 12.

Catalogue Number 25l. THE CARCERI.

An Arched Chamber with Lower Arches Surmounted by Posts and Chains. Strong Light Entering from the Right Hand.

SIGNED: lower left: Piranesi f.

NUMBERED: XII upper right.

STATE: Hind II.

F. 35. Hind 12.

Catalogue Number 24k. THE CARCERI.

Colonnaded Interior with a Broad Staircase Divided in Two by a Stone Projection with Barred Window.

SIGNED: lower right: Piranesi f.

ETCHING: H. 16″ (406 mm.) W. 21⅝″ (549 mm.)

STATE: Hind I.

F. 36. Hind 13.

Catalogue Number 25m. THE CARCERI.

Colonnaded Interior with a Broad Staircase Divided in Two by a Stone Projection with Barred Window.

SIGNED: lower right: Piranesi f.

NUMBERED: XIII upper right.

STATE: Hind II.

F. 36. Hind 13.

Catalogue Number 24l. THE CARCERI.

A Perspective of Colonnades with Zig-Zag Staircase and Two Figures on Arch Overlooking the Central Flight.

UNSIGNED.

ETCHING: H. 16³/₁₆″ (411 mm.) W. 21⅜″ (543 mm.)

STATE: Hind I.

F. 37. Hind 14.

Catalogue Number 24n. THE CARCERI.

A Wide Hall with Low Timbered Roof in the Foreground from Which Hangs a Lantern.

UNSIGNED.

ETCHING: H. 15¹⁵/₁₆″ (405 mm.) W. 21½″ (547 mm.)

STATE: Hind I.

F. 39. Hind 16.

Catalogue Number 25n. THE CARCERI.

A Perspective of Colonnades with Zig-Zag Staircase and Two Figures on Arch Overlooking the Central Flight.

SIGNED: below towards left: Piranesi F.

NUMBERED: XIV upper right.

STATE: Hind II.

F. 37. Hind 14.

Catalogue Number 25p. THE CARCERI.

A Wide Hall with Low Timbered Roof in the Foreground from Which Hangs a Lantern.

SIGNED: lower right: Piranesi F.

NUMBERED: XVI lower right.

STATE: Hind II.

F. 39. Hind 16.

Catalogue Number 24m. THE CARCERI.

Round Arches Springing from a Square Column Ornamented with the Heads of Giants with Rings in Their Mouths.

UNSIGNED.

ETCHING: H. 16⅛″ (410 mm.) W. 21½″ (547 mm.)

STATE: Hind I.

F. 38. Hind 15.

Catalogue Number 25o. THE CARCERI.

Round Arches Springing from a Square Column Ornamented with the Heads of Giants with Rings in Their Mouths.

SIGNED: lower left: Piranesi F.

NUMBERED: XV upper left.

STATE: Hind II.

F. 38. Hind 15.

Catalogue Number 26. CATALOGO.

Etched Plate:
CATALOGO DELLE OPERE/ DATE FINORA ALLA LVCE/ DA GIO. BATTISTA PIRANESI/ . . . / Si vendono presso il medesimo Autore nel palazzo del Conte Tomati a Strada Felice, vicino alla Trinità de' Monte (F. 1)

At least as early as 1761, Piranesi opened his own print publishing establishment at the Palazzo Tomati on the Strada Felice. Presumably, in 1761 he published the first state of his *Catalogo* although all states are undated. This single etched plate contains a rich frame surrounding an open area for the list of works. This first state (which lists all items thus far published) is still half blank. Each time Piranesi published a new work he added it to the *Catalogo*. Often the most recent additions were recorded in handwritten entries for a certain period of time, to be etched onto the plate at some later date. Comparison of successive states tells us the exact sequence of Piranesi's works as well as which ones appeared at the same time. The approximate dates of undated works can thus often be deduced (e.g., individual plates of the *Vedute di Roma*). The basic list of states is that compiled by Hind though many intermediate states have since come to light (Hind, p. 6).

The *Catalogo* remained in use throughout Piranesi's lifetime. By about 1770 there was no further room for new entries. A blank supplementary copper plate was then added for the growing oeuvre. The two plates — the full *Catalogo* and the overflow on the blank plate — were then combined for a single impression, so that the effect is like a caption.

Two states of the *Catalogo* occur in the Sackler Set. The earlier state, found loosely inserted in one of the volumes is intermediate between Hind (3) and (4). There are two copies of a later state. Of the two, one also was found loosely inserted in one of the volumes. The other is bound in the back of Volume IV of the *Antichità romane (Catalogue Number 35)*. The earlier state, like all *Cataloghi*, lists the works in an arbitrary arrangement. However, its entries are listed below in a chronological order.

[1] ARCHITETTVRE DIVERSE (The *Prima parte* with additions).
[2] CARCERI . . .
[3] ARCHI TRIONFALI . . .
[4] TROFEI D'OTTAVIANO . . .
[5] ANTICHITÀ ROMANE . . .
[6] DELLA MAGNIFICENZA
[7] Ritratto . . . di . . . CLEMENTE XIII.
[8] DEL CASTELLO DELL' ACQVA GIVLIA . . .
[9] FASTI CONSVLARES (Lapides Capitolini) . . .
[10] CAMPVS MARTIVS . . .
[11] DELL' EMISSARIO DEL LAGO ALBANO . . . A blank space is left for the number of plates and the price.
[12] VEDVTE DI ROMA. 60 Vedute are etched on the plate. [61], Del tempio della Sibilla in Tivoli, is added in handwritten form.

Two additions distinguish the *Catalogo* sheets of the later state from the earlier one just described. One addition is in the *Emissario* whose number of plates (9) and the price (r:50) have been penned in by hand. The other addition is to the handwrit-

ten title of plate [61] of the *Vedute* (see [12] above in description of earlier state) and in a different hand. In fact, there are two versions of this addition, although both refer to the same Temple of the Sibyl at Tivoli which appears in plate [61], and therefore correspond to *Vedute* [62] and [63] which show different views of the same temple. In the illustrated copy *(Catalogue Number 26)*, the phrase reads "3. Tavole." In the copy bound in Volume IV of the *Antichità romane (Catalogue Number 35)* the phrase reads "in 3." This later state of the *Catalogo* corresponds to Hind (4).

Catalogue Number 27. OPERE VARIE (Overall title page of Volume [I] of Sackler Set)

Letterpress title page for volume of collected early works:
OPERE VARIE / DI / ARCHITETTURA / PROSPETTIVE / GROTTESCHI / ANTICHITÀ / SUL GUSTO DEGLI ANTICHI ROMANI / *Inventate, ed Incise* / DA GIO. BATISTA PIRANESI / ARCHITETTO VENEZIANO / IN ROMA, MDCCL. / CON LICENZA DE' SUPERIORI. / Si vendono presso l'Autore nel palazzo del Signor Conte Tomati / su la strada Felice alla Trinità de' Monti.

The title page *Opere varie* with Giovanni Bouchard as publisher was first applied to a collection of Piranesi's works in 1750 according to the date there given. There were at least two later editions of this title page in Piranesi's lifetime. Hind's *Later edition A* (also published by Bouchard) and *Later edition B* (Hind, p. 78–79). They are both still dated 1750 although, in actual fact, they must be later. *Later edition B*, to which the present copy belongs, is demonstrably so since it gives Piranesi as publisher at the address to which he is supposed to have moved in 1761. The contents of the collection changed over the years. According to Hind, the first edition and the *Later edition A* contained only the revised *Prima parte* (title page and sixteen plates) plus five more. In *Later edition B*, ten more plates have been added. At least as early as the time our copy was printed, three further works were regularly included in this collected volume: the *Carceri d' invenzione*, the *Trofei di Ottaviano Augusto* and the *Antichità romane de' tempi della repubblica*. This final version became Volume [VIII] of the posthumously published collected works which were arranged by Francesco Piranesi.

CONTENTS: Letterpress title page (quoted above) printed in black and red: vignette on title page (F. 120).

WATERMARK: Not legible.

DIMENSIONS OF VOLUME: H. 24 1/32" (610 mm.) W. 17 5/16" (440 mm.)

BINDING AND CONDITION OF VOLUME: Bound in publisher's marbled boards with end papers and blank flyleaves. Leaves untrimmed. Single leaves have inner margins folded; the double leaves guarded on hinges (sometimes two on a double hinge); all arranged in gatherings and center stitched. Spine mostly gone. Disbound up to plate 1 [i.e.5] of *Antichità romane*. . . . From that point, the horizontal cords hold the gatherings in place; the back is attached and there remains part of the thin paper spine. Heavy yellow staining (damp and water) begins about plate 8 of the *Prima parte*, becomes more extensive and almost covers the leaves of the *Carceri* and *Trofei* and finally diminishes and fades away in the *Antichità romane*. Smoke (?) staining on outer edges of leaves. First few leaves show considerable wear.

GENERAL NOTE: Signed on recto of front flyleaf: *A F. R* Bound with this volume are the works described in *Catalogue Numbers 25a-n, 28, 29 and 30*.

CARCERI D'INVENZIONE (Second work in the Volume of the *Opere varie*)

The entries for this series are found with those for the *Carceri*, State II in *Catalogue Number 25a-p*

Catalogue Number 28. PRIMA PARTE (First work in the volume of the *Opere varie*)

Etched title page:
PRIMA PARTE / DI ARCHITETTURE / E PROSPETTIVE / INVENTATE ED INCISE / DA GIAMBATISTA PIRANESI / ARCHITETTO VENEZIANO / FRA GLI ARCADI / SALCINDIO TISEIO

The *Prima parte di architetture . . .* , Piranesi's first independently published work, appeared in 1743. The plates depict mostly architectural fantasies influenced by theater designers like the Bibiena family and, secondly, antique ruins close to those etched by Marco Ricci. Though the etching technique is conventional, the ideas expressed hold many portents for the future. For example, plate 2 is entitled *Carcere oscura*. It consists of an etched title page (F. 2), a two page letterpress dedication, twelve numbered plates (F. 3–4, 6, 14, 7–13, 13bis) and a letterpress list of the plates. The first edition of the *Prima parte* is very rare. One of the few known copies belongs to the Avery Library. Piranesi later revised this first effort and produced the standard version to be found in all copies of the *Opere varie*. He dropped the letterpress leaves and plate 12 (*Atrio Dorico*, F. 13bis), added five new plates (F. 5, 15–18), renumbered the original eleven, and arrived at a work consisting of the etched title and sixteen numbered plates (F. 2–18, excluding 13bis). Included with this work are the following miscellaneous plates: five small plates originally etched for the *Lettere di Giustificazione* of 1757, modified and given new titles; five further small plates of fantastic architecture; finally the four *Groteschi*, the *Pianta di ampio magnifico collegio* and the *Parte di ampio magnifico porto*.

COLLATION: Thirty-three etched plates on twenty-eight leaves (including title). Plates 1–14 only (excluding title) are numbered. Leaves [18–22] contain two small plates each. Leaves [23–28] are double plates.

CONTENTS: Etched title page (quoted above) (F. 2); leaves [2–17] (plates 1–6 [16] 7–8 [15] 9–14) [18–28] (F. 3–4, 14–15, 5–6, 18, 16, 7, 17, 8–13, 130, 129, 132, 131, 126, 125, 124, 123, 128, 127, 121, 20–22, 122, 23; Hind 1–6, 16, 7–8, 15, 9–14, 20 b & a, 21b & a, 18 b & a, 17b & a, 19b & a, 22, 24–26, 23, 27).

WATERMARKS: Hind's type 3.

DIMENSIONS OF VOLUME: See *Catalogue Number 27*.

IMPRESSIONS: The plates are printed in dark brown to black inks.

NOTES: In later states, leaves [23–28] are numbered 22, 24–26, 23, 27 respectively.

Catalogue Number 29. TROFEI DI OTTAVIANO AUGUSTO (Third work in the volume of the *Opere varie*)

Letterpress title page:
TROFEI / DI OTTAVIANO AUGUSTO / INNALZATI PER LA VITTORIA AD ACTIUM E CONQUISTA DELL'EGITTO / Con varj altri ornamenti diligentemente ricavati dagli avanzi più preziosi / delle Fabbriche antiche di Roma / UTILI A' PITTORI SCULTORI ED ARCHITETTI / DISEGNATI ED INCISI / DA GIAMBATTISTA PIRANESI ARCHITETTO VENEZIANO. / SI VENDONO IN ROMA / DA GIOVANNI BOUCHARD MERCANTE LIBRAJO SUL CORSO A S. MARCELLO / IN ROMA MDCCLIII. NELLA STAMPARIA DI GIOVANNI GENEROSO SALOMONJ ALLA PIAZZA DI S. IGNAZIO. / CON LICENZA DE' SUPERIORI.

This collection of eight plates features two double plates depicting the *Trofei di Ottaviano Augusto*. These two magnificent marble trophies date from the time of Domitian, not Augustus, and originally decorated one of his monuments. Possibly in the reign of Alexander Severus they were removed to the *Nymphaeum Aquae Iuliae*, Piranesi's *Castello dell' Acqua Giulia*. In 1590, they were moved to their present place, the balustrade of the *Piazza del Campidoglio*. The other six plates present a medley of some thirty ancient architectural fragments — capitals, friezes, decorated drums of columns, entablatures, etc.

Francesco Piranesi published a new edition which Hind says is "dated 1780 in catalogue of 1792" (Hind, p. 83).

COLLATION: Letterpress p. [1–4]. Eight unnumbered etched plates, of which Plates [1–4] are double. One etched illustration.

CONTENTS: P. [1] blank; p. [2–3] letterpress title page printed in black and red on double leaf (quoted above); p. [4] blank; vignette on title page (F. 134); plates [1–8] (F. 136.3, 137.6, 138, 139, 142, 140, 143, 141).

WATERMARKS: Title has Hind's type 1 (Colnaghi's type 5): fleur-de-lis in a circle. The rest are Hind's type 3.

DIMENSIONS OF VOLUME: See *Catalogue Number 27*.

IMPRESSIONS: The plates are printed in brown ink.

NOTES: This copy lacks the plate *Veduta dell' avanzo del Castello . . .* (F. 135) which often appears in this work and which also served as part of the *Vedute di Roma* (Hind 34).

Catalogue Number 30. ANTICHITÀ ROMANE DE'
TEMPI DELLA REPUBBLICA (Fourth work in the
volume of the *Opere varie*)

Etched title page:
ANTICHITÀ ROMANE DE' TEMPI DELLA REPUBBLICA, /
E DE' PRIMI IMPERATORI, / DISEGNATE, ED INCISE DA
GIAMBATTISTA PIRANESI / ARCHITETTO VENEZIANO:
/ E DALLO STESSO DEDICATE / ALL' ILLMO E REVMO
SIG. MONSIG. GIOVANNI BOTTARI / CAPPELLANO
SEGRETO DI N. S. BENEDETTO XIV / UNO DE CUS-
TODI DELLA BIBLIOTECA VATICANA, / E CANONICO
DI S. MARIA IN TRASTEVERE. / PARTE PRIMA / Roma si
vende dall' Auttore dirimpetto l'Academia di Franzia

*The Antichità romane de'tempi della repubblica e de'primi im-
peratori* was published by Piranesi in 1748 and offered for sale at
the artist's shop across from the French Academy in Rome. The
volume bears a dedication, dated July 20, to the famous an-
tiquarian Giovanni Bottari, librarian of the Vatican and private
chaplain to Pope Benedict XIV. At that time, Piranesi had
known Bottari for at least four years (a letter exists, dated
March 29, 1744, written from the artist in Venice to the an-
tiquarian in Rome to thank him for favors received there the
preceding year), and the dedication should most probably be
considered an acknowledgement of gratitude, rather than an
attempt to curry favor.

The first edition comprised thirty plates. These included two
unnumbered title pages, an unnumbered dedication page, two
pages of inscriptions (plates 3 and 4), twenty-six numbered
views of Roman monuments (plates 5–28), an unnumbered
view of the Arch of Gallienus. The second title page occurs
between plates 15 and 16, and plate 5 is erroneously numbered
as plate 1, a mistake which is usually corrected by hand.

The volume was reissued after 1765 as *Alcune vedute di archi
trionfali . . .* , the title by which it has become most widely
known. In this later edition, the order of the plates is changed
and two entirely new works are included, one of which is signed
by Francesco Piranesi. Although the title page of this edition is
completely different from that of the earlier one, the dedication
page from that edition is retained unchanged, still bearing the
1758 date.

The volume falls into two halves. The first of these is devoted
to monuments found within Rome itself and ends with plate 15.
The second, as its title page indicates, is devoted to monuments
outside of Rome and ranges as far afield as the Veneto and
modern Yugoslavia.

Although this set was published in 1748, it must be supposed
that work on it had been done intermittently for several years
previous to that date. The plates of the second half may date
from Piranesi's return to Venice in 1744 or 1745; or, if not
actually executed that early, must certainly be based upon
sketches made at that time.

REFERENCES: Mayor, p. 35; Hind, pp. 75–76; Fleming, pp. 180–181.

John E. Mortensen

COLLATION: Thirty etched plates (including two titles, one dedication and two
text leaves) numbered 4–3, 1[i.e. 5], 6–15, 16–28. Plates [1–2] lack numbers;
an unnumbered plate occurs between Plates 15 and 16. Another follows Plate
28.

CONTENTS: Etched title page (quoted above) (F. 41); plate [2] Dedication to
Giovanni Bottari (F. 42); plates 4–3, Text (F. 44–43); plates 1 [i.e. 5]–15 (F.
46–56); etched title page to Part Two: ANTICHITÀ ROMANE / FVORI
DI ROMA / DISEGNATE ED INCISE / DA GIAMBATTA PIRANESI /
ARCHITETTO VENEZIANO. / PARTE SECONDA / Piranesi fecit.
Roma si vende dall' Auttore dirimpetto l'Academia di Franzia (F. 57); plates
16–28 (F. 58–70); plate [29] (f. 71).

WATERMARKS: A few are Hind's type 3. Plates 1, 6, 14, 22–23, 25, 27 are of a
type recorded neither by Hind nor Colnaghi. It consists of a fleur-de-lis in a
double circle with a capital "A" below. Not all of these are fully legible but do
seem to conform to the type described.

DIMENSIONS OF VOLUME: See *Catalogue Number 27*.

IMPRESSIONS: The plates are printed in dark brown to sepia inks.

NOTES: Hind mentioned that the *Arco di Galieno* sometimes appears, unnumbered, in this edition [i.e. 1748] (Hind, p. 75).

Catalogue Number 31. VEDUTE DI ROMA (Designated
Volume [II] of Sackler Set)

Etched title page:
VEDVTE DI ROMA / DISEGNATE ED INCISE / DA GIAM-
BATTISTA PIRANESI / ARCHITETTO VE . . . ZIANO

Piranesi worked on his great series of *Vedute di Roma* throughout most of his career. He published the earliest at an unknown
date in the later 1740's. By the time of his death, he had
completed one hundred thirty-five. Later, his son, Francesco,
added two more. Only one is dated (number [75] 1766).

Piranesi sold the *Vedute* (which are unnumbered) either indi-
vidually or in sets. From around 1761 on, he issued the sets with
plates arranged in the order given in his *Catalogo*. Hind's
catalogue of the *Vedute* follows this order and assigns a number
to each item. The first known state of the *Catalogo* offered the
first fifty-nine plates. Hind concluded that in it the plate order
was roughly chronological, i.e. the order in which they had
been published (Hind p. 7). Andrew Robison, however, be-
lieves that Piranesi had classified them simply by subject for
meaningful presentation in the first *Catalogo* and the reasons he
gives seem quite convincing (Robison I, pp. 180–183 and Robison II, pp. 181–182). He then attempts to reconstruct their
chronology and succeeds in dividing the plates into four groups
that appeared in sequence. The observations below will para-
phrase some of his points.

All the known copies of the rare collection entitled *Le magnificenze di Roma*, 1751, contain among other things, the same
thirty-four *Vedute*. Hind cites three copies of this work but
Robison says he has seen yet another. It would seem that these
thirty-four were all the *Vedute* in existence in 1751. Hind numbers them as follows: 1–5, 7–9, 14–19, 28, 29, 33, 35, 37, 38, 40,
41, 43, 45–46, 49–54, 56, 58, 59. They can be further divided.

Robison describes a volume of *Vedute* in the Princeton University Library which would seem to comprise the nineteen earliest published plates of the group cited above: Hind numbers 1–4, 7–9, 14–17, 19, 35, 38, 40, 50–52, 56.

Hind cites a fourth copy of *Le magnificenze di Roma* in the Soane Museum in London which not only contains the same thirty-four plates but also two additional ones, Hind numbers 32 and 34. An identical set of thirty-six *Vedute* appeared in the Colnaghi Piranesi exhibition in 1973/74 (Colnaghi, item 21). It would thus seem that numbers 32 and 34 were the next to be published. The remaining twenty-three, then, would have been published later, sometime between the publication of Hind numbers 32 and 34 and the issuing of the first *Catalogo*. These are Hind numbers 6, 10–13, 20–27, 30–31, 36, 39, 42, 44, 47–48, 55, 57. The plates added to the *Catalogo* beginning with number 60 are, indeed, in roughly chronological order.

It is thus possible to rearrange the Sackler *Vedute* (Hind 1–63, lacking 13 and 57) chronologically into five successively published groups:
1. nineteen plates in Princeton *Vedute* volume: Hind 1–4, 7–9, 14–17, 19, 35, 38, 40, 50–52, 56;
2. fifteen remaining plates in 1751 *Magnificenze*: Hind 5, 18, 28–29, 33, 37, 41, 43, 45–46, 49, 53–54, 58–59;
3. two added plates in Soane *Magnificenze* Hind 32 and 34;
4. twenty-one remaining plates listed on first *Catalogo*: Hind 6, 10–12, 20–27, 30–31, 36, 39, 42, 44, 47–48, 55;
5. next four plates added to later *Cataloghi*: Hind 60–63.

These five groups dramatically illustrate Piranesi's stylistic development between the 1740's and the early 1760's. A word of caution is necessary, however. In sets of the *Vedute*, such as the present one, printed in the 1760's, we no longer see the earlier plates in quite their original form. This would certainly apply to groups 1–3. Two factors contribute to this distortion. First, all the present impressions are printed in brown and sepia inks richly applied — colors which Piranesi favored in the early 1760's. In their earliest states, the plates in groups 1–3 would have been less heavily printed, more usually in a black ink. Then too, most of these early plates had been reworked by the early 1760's, changing the pictorial image. Rework has been noted here on the following thirty-three plates: Hind 1, 3, 7–9, 14–19, 23, 28, 32–35, 37–38, 40–43, 45–47, 49–51, 54, 56, 58–59. Only three (Hind 23, 42, 47) belong to group 4. Generally, shadows have been added or strengthened to make the contrasts of light and dark more pronounced. In some instances, the skies have become more dramatic (as in Hind 9). Only in Hind 35 has the image been drastically changed: the Pyramid of Cestius itself has been newly etched and vastly enlarged.

COLLATION: Etched title page, frontispiece and 59 unnumbered plates. Plates [13] and [57] are lacking. Plate [59] originally bound before [58]. Volume now disbound.

CONTENTS: The list below gives title, as it appears on the plate, then the Hind plate number followed by Hind's state number. The distinguishing feature of the state is then quoted. Robison's revised catalogue of states (Robison II) has been cited only where it clearly applies.

DIMENSIONS: H. 22 1/16″ (560 mm.) W. 31 11/16″ (805 mm.)

[1] Etched title page (quoted above). H. 1, III. Address and price: Presso l' Auttore a Strada Felice nel Palazzo Tomati vicino alla Trinità de' monti. A paoli due e mezzo.

[2] Frontispiece. H. 2, III. Address and price as in plate [1].

[3] Veduta della Basilica, e Piazza di S. Pietro in Vaticano. H. 3. IV. Address and price as in plate [1].

[4] Veduta interna della Basilica di S. Pietro in Vaticano. H. 4, II. Address: Si vendono in Roma dai SS.re Bouchard e Gravier Mercanti libraj al corso presso S. Marcello.

[5] VEDUTA DELL' ESTERNO DELLA GRAN BASILICA DI S. PIETRO IN VATICANO . . . H. 5, III. Address and price as in plate [1].

[6] Veduta della Basilica di S. Paolo fuor delle mura. H. 6, III. Address and price as in plate [1].

[7] Spaccato interno della Basilica di S. Paolo fuori delle mura . . . H. 7, III. Address and price as in plate [1].

[8] Vedute della Basilica di S. Giovanni Laterano . . . H. 8, III. Address and price as in plate [1].

[9] Veduta della Basilica di Sta. Maria Maggiore con le due Fabbriche laterali di detta Basilica . . . H. 9, III. Address and price as in plate [1].

[10] Veduta della Facciata di dietro della Basilica di S. Maria Maggiore. H. 10, II. Address and price: Presso l'Autore a Strada Felice vicino alla Trinità de' Monti. A paoli due e mezzo.

[11] Veduta della Facciata della Basilica di S. Croce in Gerusalemme. H. 11, II. Address and price as in plate [1].

[12] Veduta della Basilica di S. Lorenzo fuor delle mura. H. 12, II. Address and price: Presso l'Autore. A paoli due e mezzo.

[14] Veduta della Piazza del Popolo. H. 14, Robison D. With Piranesi's address and price as in plate [10] but with reference number "1" now roman rather than arabic.

[15] Veduta della Piazza di Monte Cavallo. H. 15, IV. Address and price as in plate [10] plus further work on the plate.

[16] Veduta di Piazza Navona sopra le rovine del Circo Agonale. H. 16, IV. Address and price as in plate [1]. Same as Robison E which describes the further reworking.

[17] Veduta della Piazza della Rotonda. H. 17, III. Address and price as in plate [1]. Before strengthening of shading, etc., described in H. IV and Robison D.

[18] Veduta di Piazza di Spagna. H. 18, IV. Address and price as in plate [1]. Same as Robison E which describes the further reworking.

[19] Veduta della vasta Fontana di Trevi anticamente detta l'Acqua Vergine. H. 19, Robison C. With Piranesi's address and price as in plate [1] but before rework of H. III. The sculpture on the fountain is still that of H. I; the statue of Neptune in central niche has his arms at his sides; the statue in front niche (left facing the fountain) is a male figure with right arm extended. Later, Piranesi changed the sculpture — H. III or Robison D. H. II consists only of minor additional shading.

[20] Veduta del Castello dell' Acqua Felice . . . H. 20, II. Address and price: Presso l'Autore. A paoli due e mezzo.

[21] Veduta del Castello dell' Acqua Paola sul Monte Aureo. H. 21, II. Address and price as in plate [10].

[22] Veduta del Palazzo fabbricato sul Quirinale per le Segreterie de Brevi e della Sacra Consulta . . . H. 22, II. Address and price as in plate [1].

[23] Veduta della Gran Curia Innocenziana edificata sulle rovine dell'

Anfiteatro di Statilio Tauro, che formano l' odierno Monte Citorio . . . H. 23, I. Address and price as in plate [1].

[24] VEDUTA, nella Via del Corso, DEL PALAZZO DELL' AC-CADEMIA istituita da LUIGI XIV . . . H. 24, II. Address and price as in plate [1].

[25] Veduta sul Monte Quirinale del Palazzo dell' Eccellentissima Casa Barberini . . . H. 25, II. Address and price as in plate [1].

[26] Veduta del Palazzo Odescalchi. H. 26, II. Address and price as in plate [1].

[27] Veduta del Porto di Ripa Grande. H. 27, II. Address and price as in plate [1].

[28] Veduta del Porto di Ripetta. H. 28, IV. Address and price as in plate [1].

[29] Veduta del Ponte e Castello Sant' Angelo. H. 29, II. Address and price as in plate [1].

[30] VEDUTA del Mausoleo d'Elio Adriano (ora chiamato Castello S. Angelo) . . . H. 30, I. Address and price as in plate [10].

[31] Veduta del Ponte Salario. H. 31, II. Address and price as in plate [1].

[32] Veduta della Dogana di Terra a Piazza di Pietra. H. 32, III. Address and price as in plate [1].

[33] TEATRO DI MARCELLO . . . H. 33, Robison C. Address and price as in plate [1]. Strengthening of many minor lines of shading on left half of Teatro.

[34] Veduta dell avanzo del Castello, che prendendo una porzione dell' Acqua Giulia . . . H. 34, III. Address and price as in plate [1].

[35] Veduta del Sepolcro di Cajo Cestio. H. 35, III. Address and price as in plate [1].

[36] Piramide di C. Cestio. H. 36, I. Address: Presso l'Autore.

[37] VEDUTA INTERNA DEL SEPOLCRO DI S. COSTAN-ZA . . . H. 37, III. Address and price as in plate [10].

[38] Veduta del Romano Campidoglio con Scalinata. H. 38, II. Address and price as in plate [1].

[39] Veduta del Campidoglio di fianco. H. 39, II. Address: Presso l'Autore. Before further work on plate.

[40] Veduta di Campo Vaccino. H. 40, III. Address and price as in plate [1].

[41] Veduta del Sito, ov' era l'antico Foro Romano . . . H. 41, III. Address and price: Presso l'Autore. A due paoli e mezzo.

[42] Veduta degli avanzi del Foro di Nerva. H. 42, III. Address and price as in plate [1].

[43] VEDUTA DEL PIANO SUPERIORE DEL SERRAGLIO DELLE FIERE FABBRICATO DA DOMIZIANO. H. 43, III. Address and price as in plate [10].

[44] Veduta del Tempio di Giove Tonante. H. 44, II. Address and price as in plate [10].

[45] VEDUTA DEGLI AVANZI DEL TABLINO DELLA CASA AUREA DI NERONE, DETTI VOLGARMENTE IL TEMPIO DELLA PACE. H. 45, III. Address and price as in plate [10]. Before rework added in Robison D.

[46] Veduta del Tempio della Fortuna virile. H. 46, III. Address and price as in plate [1].

[47] Veduta del Tempio di Cibele a Piazza della Bocca della Verità. H. 47, II. Address and price as in plate [10].

[48] Veduta del Tempio di Bacco, inoggi Chiesa di S. Urbano...H. 48, II. Address and price as in plate [1].

[49] Veduta del Tempio d'Antonino e Faustina in Campo Vaccino. H. 49, III. Address and price as in plate [1].

[50] Veduta degli avanzi di due Triclinj che appartenevano alla Casa aurea di Nerone, presi erroneamente per i Templi del Sole, e della Luna, o d'Iside, e Serapide. H. 50, state falls between Robison C and D. Address and price as in plate [1] but before diagonal shadow across facade between two niches and other shading.

[51] Colonna Trajana. H. 51, IV. Address and price as in plate [1] and with shading at end of column heavily rebitten.

[52] Colonna Antonina. H. 52, III. Address and price as in plate [1].

[53] OBELISCO EGIZIO . . . H. 53, state falls between Robison B and C. Piranesi's address and price as in plate [1] but before the added work in the foreground (i.e., the man on the farthest right casts no shadow).

[54] Arco di Settimio Severo. H. 54, Robison D. Address and price as in plate [1]. Short heavy horizontals added on ground to left of boulder above "Piranesi . . . (etc.)"

[55] Veduta dell' Arco di Tito. H. 55, I. Address and price as in plate [10].

[56] Veduta dell' Arco di Costantino . . . H. 56, III. Address and price as in plate [10].

[58] Veduta dell' Atrio del Portico di Ottavia. H. 58, IV. Address and price as in plate [10].

[59] Veduta interna dell' Atrio del Portico di Ottavia. H. 59, III. Address and price as in plate [10].

[60] Veduta del Pantheon d'Agrippa oggi Chiesa di S. Maria ad Martyres. H. 60, I. Address and price: Si Vendono paoli tre presso il medesimo Autore nel palazzo del Conte Tomati.

[61] Veduta del tempio della Sibilla in Tivoli. H. 61, I. Address and price as in plate [1].

[62] ALTRA VEDVTA DEL TEMPIO DELLA SIBILLA IN TIVOLI. H. 62, I. No address (horizontal format).

[63] Altra Veduta del tempio della Sibilla in Tivoli. H. 63, I. No address (vertical format).

WATERMARKS: Hind's type 3.

IMPRESSIONS: Plates printed in inks which range from almost black through browns and sepias, some quite golden. Plates [4] and [9] are printed in black ink.

BINDING AND CONDITION: Bound in publisher's marbled wrappers with end papers but no flyleaves. Leaves untrimmed and unfolded, being simply side stitched with no gatherings. No spine. Disbound. Staining on front cover at top and bottom near the center affecting also the first thirteen leaves. Water-staining in right margin of first six leaves. Plate [27] has an old repair: vertical strip of paper pasted on the verso of lower right margin. Plate [38] has the same in upper left margin.

NOTES: All the plates which mention address give Piranesi as the publisher, most of them with his address at the Palazzo Tomati on the Strada Felice. Only plate [4] is in an earlier state. It gives Bouchard and Gravier as publishers. Signed on title page: A.F.R.

Catalogue Number 32. ANTICHITÀ ROMANE, Volume I (Designated Volume [III] of the Sackler Set)

Letterpress title page:

LE ANTICHITÀ / ROMANE / OPERA / DI GIAMBATISTA / PIRANESI / ARCHITETTO VENEZIANO / DIVISA IN QUATTRO TOMI / NEL PRIMO DE' QUALI SI CONTEN-GONO / GLI AVANZI DEGLI ANTICHI EDIFIZJ DI ROMA / DISPOSTI IN TAVOLA TOPOGRAFICA / SECONDO L'ODIERNA LORO ESISTENZA / ED ILLUSTRATI CO' FRAMMENTI DELL' ANTICA ICNOGRAFIA MARMOREA, / E CON UN INDICE CRITICO DELLA LORO DE-NOMINAZIONE / ARRICHITO DI TAVOLE SUPPLETORIE / FRALLE QUALI SI DIMOSTRANO / *L'elevazione degli stressi avanzi: l'andamento degli antichi Aquedotti nelle vicinanze e nel dentro / di Roma, correlativo al Commentario Frontiniano ivi esposto in compendio: la Pianta / delle Terme le più cospicue: del Foro Romano colle Contrade circon-vicine: / del Monte Capitolino: ed altre le più riguardevoli.* / NEL SECON-DO, E NEL TERZO / *Gli Avanzi de' Monumenti Sepolcrali esistenti in Roma, e nell' Agro Romano colle loro / rispettive piante, elevazioni, sezioni, vedute esterne ed interne: colla dimostrazione / de' sarcofagi, ceppi, vasi cenerarj e unguentarj, bassirilievi, stucchi, / musaici, iscrizioni, e tutt' altro ch' è stato in essi ritrovato: / e colle loro indicazioni e spiegazioni.* / NEL QUARTO / *I Ponti antichi di Roma che inoggi sono in essere, colle Vestigia dell' antica Isola / Tiberina, gli Avanzi de' Teatri, de' Portici, e di altri Monumenti, / eziandio colle loro indicazioni e spiegazioni.* / TOMO PRIMO. / IN ROMA, MDCCLVI. / NELLA STAMPERIA DI ANGELO ROTILJ / NEL PALAZZO DE' MASSIMI. / CON LICENZA DE' SUPERIORI. / SI VENDONO IN ROMA DAI SIGNORI BOUCHARD E GRAVIER MERCANTI LIBRAJ AL CORSO / PRESSO SAN MARCELLO.

In 1752 Piranesi began what was to become his most ambitious project, *Le Antichità romane*. The work was originally to be entitled *Monumenta Sepulcralia Antiqua*, and was to deal exclusively with the tombs, inscriptions and the "urne cippi e vasi cenerari" that obsessed Piranesi's imagination. Foreseeing the difficulties of financing an undertaking of such scope, Piranesi sought out patronage. From Pope Benedict XIV he received permission to import two hundred bales of paper duty-free. He also received a promise of patronage from James Caulfield, Viscount Charlemont, a young Irish nobleman, *dilettante* and *gran turista*. Having been assured of financial backing, Piranesi expanded his original conception to incorporate all types of Roman antiquities, including aqueducts, theaters and bridges. The master worked on the *Antichità* for four years, and despite setbacks such as the failure of Charlemont's patronage it was printed at the stamperia of Angelo Rotili and published in Rome by Bouchard on May 9, 1756. The four folio volumes contain over two hundred fifty plates. As valuable a tool as it was upon publication, being the most comprehensive pictorial collection of Roman antiquities ever produced, it is even more so today. Not only has it never been equalled, but over one-half the monuments it represents have been lost or further damaged since Piranesi's time. The enthusiastic reception which the *Antichità* received throughout Europe was demonstrated by Piranesi being made an honorary member of the Society of Antiquaries in London on February 24, 1757, less than ten months after the publication of this remarkable work.

REFERENCES: *Fine Old Master Drawings*, Christie, Mansen and Woods, London, March 30, 1971.

Martin Filler

COLLATION: Letterpress p. [1–2, 1–4] 1–40, I–XI, i–iii, i–iv, i–iii [1–2]. Eight etched illustrations in text (including initials). Etched frontispiece and seventy four etched plates on forty four leaves numbered I–XLIIII. Plate leaves VIII–XXXVII contain two plates per leaf (i.e. VIII, I and [VIII] II). Plates I–V and XLIII are double. Plates VI and VII are single but have very wide inner margins and have been folded twice. Plate XXXVIII is double folded (two double plates pasted together and folded three times).

CONTENTS: Frontispiece (portrait of Piranesi by Polanzani); p. [1] letterpress title page (quoted above); p. [2] blank; plate I (F. 144) second frontispiece; p. [1–4] (✝ 2): [1–2] PREFAZIONE / AGLI STUDIOSI DELLE AN-TICHITÀ ROMANE; [3] IMPRIMATUR / . . . / 25. Gennaro 1756.; [4] List of Piranesi's works: initial on p. [1] (F. 145); plates II–VII (F. 153–156); p. 1–40 ([A]–[U]): INDICE / O SIA SPIEGAZIONE DELLE VESTIGIA DI ROMA ANTICA, DELINEATA NELL' ANTEPOSTA TAVOLA TOP-OGRAFICA: vignette at head of p. 1 (F. 151); initial on p. I (F. 146): vignette on p. 2 (F. 152); p. I–XI [XII] blank (A–F): I–VII, SPIEGAZIONE / DELLA PREPOSTA TAVOLA DEGLI AQUEDOTTI; VIII–XI, OS-SERVAZIONI / Sulla determinazione de' limiti del Campo Marzio compreso nell stessa Tavola / degli Aquedotti: initial on p. I (F. 147); initial on p. VIII (F. 148); plates VIII, I–[XXXVII] II, XXXVIII (F. 157–217); p. i–iii [iv blank] (a–b): INDICE, O SIA SPIEGAZIONE / DELL' ANTEPOSTA TAVOLA DELLE TERME DI CARACALLA: initial on p. i. (F. 149); plates XXXIX–XLI (F. 218–220); p. i–iv (a–b): INDICE / DELL' AN-TEPOSTA TAVOLA DEL FORO ROMANO, E DELLE CONTRADE / COMPRESE NELLA MEDESIMA; plates XLII–XLIII (F. 221–222); p. i–iii [iv blank] (*.**): INDICE / DELL' ANTEPOSTA TAVOLA DEL MONTE CAPITOLINO: initial on p. i. (F. 150); plate XLIIII (F. 223); p. [1–2]: REPERTORIO / Degli Avanzi delle Antiche Fabbriche di Roma / denominati in questo primo Tomo.

WATERMARKS: Hind's type 3.

DIMENSIONS: H. 23½" (590 mm.) W. 17⅛" (435 mm.)

IMPRESSIONS: The plates are printed in dark brown to sepia inks.

BINDING AND CONDITION: Bound in publisher's marbled boards with end papers and blank flyleaves. Leaves untrimmed. Leaves guarded on folded hinges or with folded inner margins, arranged in gatherings and center stitched. Thin paper spine mostly missing. Disbound, but with remains of horizontal cords. Considerable foxing in pages 1–40.

NOTES: Signed on title page: *Joh: Richards / given to A. & F. Richards / Jan.* 1808– Imprimatur, dated: 25. Gennaro 1756. List of Piranesi's works, p. [4]: *Opere finora date in luce dall' Autore, e loro rispettivi prezzi, i a' quali si vendono in Roma / DAI SIG. BOUCHARD, E GRAVIER / MERCANTI LIBRAJ. / I presenti quattro Volumi: al prezzo di Zecchini quindici. / Vedute di Roma in foglio atlantico, carta papale, date finora in luce sino al nume- / ro di trentanove: al prezzo di due paoli, e mezzo l'una. / Prospettive inventate sulla maniera degli antichi Romani, con varj grotteschi in carta pa- / pale, foglio atlantico: al prezzo di paoli quaranta. / Carceri parimente d'invenzione in carta papale, foglio atlantico: al prezzo di paoli quat- / tordici. / Vedute di Antichità Romane, si di Roma, che dell'Italia in trenta fogli, carta papale: / al prezzo di paoli sedici. / Trofei d'Ottaviano Augusto, con altri antichi ornamenti d'Architettura, carta papale, / foglio atlantico: al prezzo di paoli ventitrè.* In line [7] the phrase "è mezzo l'una" is a handwritten correction. [Plate XVII] II trimmed to border and pasted over an impression of another plate in series printed there by error. [Plates XXXV] II and [XXXIIII] II (F. 212 & 210) printed in reverse order.

Catalogue Number 33. ANTICHITÀ ROMANE, Volume II (Designated Volume [IV] of the Sackler Set)

Etched title page:

LE ANTICHITÀ / ROMANE / DI GIAMBATISTA PIRANESI / ARCHITETTO VENEZIANO / TOMO SECONDO / CON-TENENTE GLI AVANZI / DE' MONVMENTI / SEPOL-CRALI / DI ROMA E DELL' AGRO ROMANO / Piranesi f.

COLLATION: Sixty-three etched plates (including title, frontispiece and index) numbered I–LXIII. Plates II, VII, IX–X, XII–XXII, XXIV–XXV, XXVIII, XXX, XXXII–XXXV, XXXVII, XXXIX–XLII, XLIV–XLVII,

XLIX–LVIII, LXII–LXIII are double. Plate V is double folded (two double plates pasted together and folded five times).

CONTENTS: Plate I, etched title page (quoted above); plate II, frontispiece; Tav. III / INDICE / DEL CONTENVTO / IN QVESTO SECONDO TOMO / E NEL TERZO; plate IV–LXIII (F. 224–285.)

WATERMARKS: Hind's type 3.

DIMENSIONS: H. 23³/₁₆″ (589 mm.) W. 17⅛″ (435 mm.)

IMPRESSIONS: The plates are printed in dark brown to sepia inks.

BINDING AND CONDITION: Bound in publisher's marbled boards with end papers and blank flyleaves. Leaves untrimmed. Single leaves have inner margins folded; double leaves guarded on hinges (two per double hinge); all are arranged in gatherings and center stitched. Spine missing. Disbound, but with remains of horizontal cords. Some water staining in lower margins affecting plates LVII–LXIII.

NOTES: Signed on recto of front flyleaf: A F.R. Jean Barbault (1705?–1766) etched the figures in plates XII–XV, XX, XXXIII, XXXV, XLV–XLVI. They have added signatures: *Barbault scolpi figure* or *Barbault scolpi le Fig.* Plate XXXIV is unsigned and in outline without shading. It hardly seems worthy of Piranesi. Plate LX has this pencil inscription: *L.H 1789 lost Sept. / found Jan.ry 3rd 1790*

Catalogue Number 34. ANTICHITÀ ROMANE, Volume III (Designated Volume [V] of the Sackler Set)

Etched title:
LE ANTICHITÀ / ROMANE / DI GIAMBATISTA PIRANESI / ARCHITETTO VENEZIANO / TOMO QVARTO / CONTENENTE I PONTI ANTICHI / GLI AVANZI DE' TEATRI / DE' PORTICI / E DI ALTRI MONVMENTI / DI ROMA / Piranesi Arch. inv. e scolp.

COLLATION: Fifty-four etched plates (including title and frontispiece) numbered I–LIV. Plates II–III, VI, VIII–XV, XVIII–XIX, XXI–XXXVII, XXXIX–XL, XLII, XLV–LIV are double. Plate XLI is double folded (two plates, one double, pasted together and folded five times).

CONTENTS: Plate I, etched title page (quoted above); plate II, frontispiece; plates III–LIV (F. 286–336).

WATERMARKS: Hind's type 3.

DIMENSIONS: H. 23¹/₃₂″ (585 mm.) W. 17⁵/₁₆″ (440 mm.)

IMPRESSIONS: The plates printed in dark brown to sepia inks.

BINDING AND CONDITION: Bound in publisher's marbled boards with end papers and blank flyleaves. Leaves untrimmed. Single leaves have inner margins folded; double leaves guarded on hinges; all are arranged in gatherings and center stitched. Spine missing. Disbound, but with remains of horizontal cords.

NOTES: Signed on recto of front flyleaf: A F.R. Jean Barbault (1705?–1766) etched the figures in plates XXVII–XXIX, XLVI, XLVIII. They have added signatures: *Barbault scolpi le Fig.e* or *Barbault scolpi le Figure.* Plate XXV is signed: *Girolamo Rossi sculp.* Plates XXIV and XXVI are signed: *Antonio Buonamici delin. Girolamo Rossi Sculp.* Thieme-Becker lists a Girolamo Rossi II as a Roman engraver, 1682–after 1762, who may be the same man whose work appears here. Antonio Buonamici is not listed in Thieme–Becker. Plate XXIII is unsigned but closely resembles XXIV and XXVI. Plates XXIII and XXIV have captions printed from narrow separate plates. In Focillon's list (F. 308 [1]–308 [2]) these captions occur in reverse order to that in the present copy. Focillon's order appears in another copy in Avery Library (AE/659/P662/v.3) which is a late 18th century printing. It would seem that the arrangement in the Sackler copy is the correct one. The caption below plate XXIV speaks of "una gran Cassa di marmo egregiam te scolpita, nel mez-/zo appariscono le tre Grazie . . ." This marble chest with the three Graces does indeed appear in the view above. Plate XXI is an unsigned plan, surely not by Piranesi.

Catalogue Number 35. ANTICHITÀ ROMANE, Volume IV (Designated Volume [VI] of the Sackler Set)

Etched title:
LE ANTICHITÀ / ROMANE / DI GIAMBATISTA PIRANESI / ARCHITETTO VENEZIANO / TOMO QVARTO / CONTENENTE I PONTI ANTICHI / GLI AVANZI DE' TEATRI / DE' PORTICI / E DI ALTRI MONVMENTI / DI ROMA / Piranesi Arch. inv. e scolp.

COLLATION: Fifty-seven etched plates (including title, frontispiece and index) numbered I–LVII. Plates II, IV, IX–XII, XV–XXIII, XXVII, XXXII, XXXIX–XLIII, LIII are double. Double folded are plates VI (two double plates pasted together and folded four times), VII and XXVIII (the same; folded five times), XXIX–XXX (each with two plates, one double, pasted together and folded five times).

CONTENTS: Plate I, etched title page (quoted above); plate II, frontispiece; Tav. III / INDICE / DEL / CONTENVTO / IN QVESTO QVARTO TOMO; plates IV–LVII (F. 337–340, 344–345, 342–341, 343, 346–368, 370–379, 381, 383–395).

WATERMARKS: Hind's type 3; plate LVI has watermark close to Colnaghi 8.

DIMENSIONS: H. 23¼″ (590 mm.) W. 17⁷/₁₆″ (443 mm.)

IMPRESSIONS: The plates are printed in dark brown to sepia inks.

BINDING AND CONDITION: Bound in publisher's marbled paper boards with end papers and blank flyleaves. Leaves untrimmed. Some single leaves have inner margins folded. These folded margins serve as hinges onto which other single or double leaves are guarded; all are arranged in gatherings and center stitched. Spine missing. Disbound, but with remains of horizontal cords. Staining in upper margins from front flyleaf to plate VII and from plate XXIV to the end of flyleaf. Tear on plate XLIII has been patched with a small piece of paper on the lower left corner, verso.

NOTES: Signed on recto of front flyleaf: A F R. Plates VI–X in the present copy were, according to Focillon, numbered IX–X, VII, VI, VIII respectively in their earliest impressions. Focillon attributes our numbering to the second edition, 1784. The three new plates of the second edition (F. 369, 380 and 382) had not yet been produced at the time our copy was printed. This is an example of the casual manner in which volumes of engravings were revised in the 18th century. Already, presumably in the early 1760's, four plates had been renumbered. Then, at some unknown time, three new plates were added. Finally, in 1784, a new frontispiece and dedication completed work on the new edition. A copy of Piranesi's *Catalogo delle opere* . . . is bound in after plate LVII. Its folded inner margin serves as a hinge onto which plate LVII is guarded (see notes under *Catalogo*).

Catalogue Number 36. LAPIDES CAPITOLINI (Designated Part I, Volume [VII] of the Sackler Set)

Etched title page:
I.B / PIRANESII / LAPIDES / CAPITOLINI / SIVE / FASTI CONSVLARES / TRIVMPHALESQ ROMANORVM / AN VRBE CONDITA / VSQVE AD TIBERIVM / CAESAREM / Piranesi F. Veneunt apud Auctorem in aedibus Comitis Thomati via Felici prope templum SS. Trinitatis in Monte Pincio.

The *Fasti Consulares* and *Fasti Triumphales* which together constitute the *Lapides Capitolini* are fragments of inscriptions originally carved on the arch of Augustus in the Roman Forum. The first lists the Consuls and higher officials of the City of Rome from its beginning up to A.D. 13. The second lists all the Triumphs celebrated in Rome up to 19 B.C. They were discovered in 1546/47 and installed in their present location in the Palazzo dei Conservatori in 1586. Piranesi depicts the inscriptions according to his own imaginary and decorative arrangement on one vast etched plate. This text consists of a preface, the completed lists with commentary and three indices of Consuls. The work dates from 1761–62.

COLLATION: Letterpress p. [1–2, 1–4] 1–61. Etched title page, dedication leaf and one unnumbered plate which is double folded (two double plates pasted together plus two narrow caption plates pasted along the lower margin; the whole thing folded five times). Four etched illustrations in the text.

CONTENTS: P. [1] half-title; p. [2] blank; etched title page (quoted above) (F. 421); dedication: CLEMENTI XIII. PON. O.M. / . . . / Piranesi F. (F. 422); p. [1–4] (a–a2): [1–4] PRAEFATIO; [4] APPROBATIO / . . . / 16. Junii 1761; vignette on p. [1] (F. 423); large unnumbered plate (F. 427); p. 1–61 ([62] blank) (A–P2 [Q]): 1–37, FASTI CONSULARES / ROMANORUM . . . ; 38, NOTAE / QVAE OCCVRRVNT IN FASTIS . . . ; 39–46, TRIVMPHI ROMANORVM / VSQVE . . . ; 47–61, INDEX / CONSVLVM . . . ; 61, ROMAE MDCCLXII. / TYPIS GENEROSI SALOMONI . . . ; vignette on p. 37 (F. 424); vignette on p. 46 (F. 425); tail-piece on p. 61 (F. 426).

WATERMARKS: None legible.

DIMENSIONS: H. 24⁷/₃₂″ (615 mm.) W. 17¾″ (450 mm.)

IMPRESSIONS: In all three works bound in this volume, the plates are printed in dark browns to sepia inks.

BINDING AND CONDITION OF VOLUME: Bound in publisher's marbled boards with end papers and blank flyleaves. Leaves untrimmed. For the most part, the three works in this volume are made up of double leaves arranged in gatherings and center stitched. These double leaves are always composed of two single leaves pasted together (one leaf with its inner margin folded, the folded margin serving as hinge onto which its mate is guarded). The double plates in *Emissario del Lago Albano* are guarded on double hinges (two plates per hinge). Spine missing. Disbound, but with remains of the horizontal cords. Considerable water staining in upper part of text leaves of *Lapides Capitolini*.

NOTES: Signed on recto of front flyleaf: A.F.R — The imprimatur (p.4) is dated June 16, 1761. Page 61 is dated Rome 1762 "typis Generosi Salomoni." Page 61 has been pasted to page 1 of *Del Castello dell' Acqua Giulia*, whose half-title and etched title united complete the signature. Bound with this are the works described in *Catalogue Number 37* and *Catalogue Number 38*.

Catalogue Number 37. LE ROVINE DEL CASTELLO (Designated Part II, Volume [VII] of the Sackler Set)

Etched title page:
LE ROVINE DEL CASTELLO / DELL' ACQVA GIVLIA / SITVATO IN ROMA PRESSO / S. EVSEBIO E FALSAMENT[E] / DETTO DELL' ACQVA MARCIA / COLLA DICHIARAZIONE DI VNO / DE' CELEBRI PASSI / DEL COMENTARIO FRONTINIANO / E SPOSIZIONE DELLA MANIERA / CON CVI GLI ANTICHI ROMANI DISTRIBVIVAN / LE ACQVE PER VSO DELLA CITTÀ / DI GIO BATISTA / PIRANESI /.../ Si / vendono / presso / l'Autore / alla Trinità / de' Monti / Piranesi F.

Piranesi is here mainly concerned with the ruins of the monumental fountain which terminate a branch of the aqueduct called *Acqua Iulia* and stand in what is now the Piazza

Vittorio Emanuele II. Its ancient title was the *Nymphaeum Aquae Iuliae*.

The facade, dating from the reign of Alexander Severus (A.D. 222–235) features a large central niche with arched openings on either side of it. In the latter stood two marble trophies which Piranesi featured in the *Trofei di Ottaviano Augusto*, of 1753. The *Rovine* was printed in 1761.

COLLATION: Letterpress p. [1–2] 1–26. Etched title page and twenty plates on eighteen leaves numbered I–XIX. Plates IV and [IV bis] are two small plates on one leaf. Tav. XVII–XVIII are also printed on the same leaf. Four etched illustrations in text (include initials).

CONTENTS: P. [1] half-title; p. [2] blank; etched title page (quoted above) (F. 396). P. 1–26 (A–F3): 1–12, DEL CASTELLO / DELL' ACQUA GIULIA; 13–20, SPIEGAZIONE / DELLE TAVOLE DEL CASTELLO / DELL' ACQUA GIULIA; 20, IMPRIMATUR (undated); 21–26, DELLE CAUTELE / USATE DAGLI ANTICHI / NELLA CONCESSIONE E DISTRIBUZIONE / DELLE ACQUE; 26, IN ROMA MDCCLXI. / NELLA STAMPERIA DI GENEROSO SALOMONI . . . ; initial on p. 1 (F. 397); tail-piece on p. 12 (F. 399); tail-piece on p. 20 (F. 400); initial on p. 21 (F. 398); plates I–XIX (F. 401–420).

WATERMARKS: Hind's type 3.

NOTES: Page 26 has date 1761 "*nella stamperia de Generoso Salomoni.*"

Catalogue Number 38. DESCRIZIONE E DISEGNO DELL' EMISSARIO (Designated Part III of Volume [VII] of the Sackler Set)

Etched title page:
DESCRIZIONE / E DISEGNO / DELL' EMISSARIO / DEL LAGO / ALBANO / DI GIO BATISTA / PIRANESI / Piranesi F.

Lake Albano lies some thirteen miles southeast of Rome and has been a favorite summer retreat for wealthy Romans since late Republican times. Situated at the bottom of an extinct crater which lacks adequate natural drainage the lake is, therefore, highly susceptible to rapid flooding during periods of heavy rainfall. For this reason, an artificial system of drainage was created in early times, in the form of a tunnel dug under the Alban Hills at the southwest corner of the lake.

This drainage tunnel, or *emissario* in Italian, is the subject of this volume by Piranesi. It is approximately one mile long, six feet high, and four feet across. It is covered by a continuous barrel vault, and the flow of water through it is controlled by a simple wooden sluice at its point of juncture with the lake.

According to Livy, the construction of the *emissario* was connected with the Roman conquest of the Etruscan city of Veii. Victory over this city was important for Rome's early expansion over the Italian peninsula. The Delphic Oracle has signified that Veii would be taken only when the level of the lake had been lowered. This was done, and the city fell. According to this source, the date of construction of the *emissario* would be between 398 and 397 B.C. It is still in use today.

The inlet to the *emissario* from the lake lies very close to Castel Gandolfo. Legrand reports that Piranesi undertook a study of it to satisfy the curiosity of Clement XIII, who was in the habit of taking the artist with him during his summer withdrawals from Rome. Piranesi's motives in publishing this volume on the *emissario* were, however, probably more complex. He had already included an illustration of it (Plate XXX) in his *Della magnificenza . . .* of 1761. In the text to that volume (p. lxxiii), Piranesi cites both the *cloaca maxima* and the *emissario* as examples of Etruscan pre-eminence over the Greeks in the building of "arched," i.e., vaulted, structures. He acknowledges that the *emissario* was too late in date to be of Etruscan origin, but insists that it follows the Etruscan structural tradition. Thus, this volume devoted entirely to the *emissario* may be considered an extension of *Della magnificenza . . .* and a continuation of Piranesi's dispute with Mariette over the relative values of Greek and Roman architecture.

John E. Mortensen

COLLATION: Letterpress p. 1–19 [20]. Etched title page and nine plates numbered I–IX. Plates I–II, IV–VII and IX are double. Plate III is double folded (two plates, one double, pasted together and folded 3 times). Two etched illustrations in the text (including an initial).

CONTENTS: Etched title page (quoted above) (F. 480); p. 1–19 [20] (A–[E2]): 1–13, DESCRIZIONE / E DISEGNO / DELL' EMISSARIO / DEL LAGO ALBANO; 14, blank; 15–19, SPIEGAZIONE / DELLE TAVOLE / DELL'EMISSARIO / DEL LAGO ALBANO; [20] IMPRIMATUR / . . . / APPROBATIO / . . . / I. Aprilis 1762; initial on p. 1 (F. 481); tail-piece on p. 13 (F. 482); plates I–IX (F. 483–491).

WATERMARKS: Hind's type 3.

CONDITION: Tear on plate VI of the *Emissario del Lago Albano* has been patched with piece of paper (70 mm.) in upper right margin.

NOTES: The *Approbatio* on p. [20] is dated April 1, 1762.

Catalogue Number 39. ANTICHITÀ D' ALBANO (Designated Part I of Volume [VIII] of Sackler Set)*

Etched title page:
ANTICHITÀ D'ALBANO / E DI CASTEL GANDOLFO / DESCRITTE ED INCISE / DA / GIOVAMBATISTA / PIRANESI / In Roma l'anno 1764.

CONTENTS: Half-title [verso blank] and etched title page only (quoted above) (F. 505).

WATERMARK: Not legible.

DIMENSIONS OF VOLUME: H. 23¹³/₁₆″ (605 mm.) W. 17¹⁵/₁₆″ (455 mm.)

IMPRESSIONS: With two exceptions, all the plates in this composite volume are printed in a black ink of moderate heaviness. The exceptions are the vignette on page [1] of *Di due spelonche* which is glowing and golden and plate XI of the same work which is in sepia.

*The volume has been opened for exhibition to the title page of the *Antichità di Cora*. Therefore, this page will not be seen. Bound with this are the works described in *Catalogue Number 40* and *Catalogue Number 41*.

BINDING AND CONDITION OF VOLUME: Bound in publisher's marbled boards with endpapers and blank flyleaves. Leaves untrimmed and, with some exceptions, entirely unfolded, being simply side stitched with no gatherings. Plates of this volume which are double plates are guarded onto a hinge which is penetrated by the side stitching. No spine. Considerable smoke (?) staining of the outer edges of the leaves.

NOTES: Signed on recto of front flyleaf: A.F.R. The composition of the present volume and of Volume [VII] differs from what later became standard. Piranesi's *Catalogo* in states issued before 1769 already list: *ANTICHITÀ D' ALBANO, E DI CASTEL GANDOLFO un volume in foglio Atlantico, in 55. Tav . . .* This stands for the *Antichità d'Albano*, the *Emissario del lago Albano*, and the *Di due spelonche*. These three works were normally bound together from then on and became Volume XI in the posthumous collected works arranged by Francesco Piranesi. The *Lapides Capitolini*, the *Antichità di Cora* and the *Castello dell' Acqua Giulia* were also customarily bound together at least as early as this standardization of the collected works of which they constitute Volume [IX]. It seems likely that the three works united in Sackler Volume [VII] were so bound because they alone of the six had been published when the Sackler set was made up. This would seem to have been about 1763. The present volume [VIII] seems to be an addition to the main set, a group of newly published works bound up and bought about 1764, with only the half-title and etched title of the *Antichità d' Albano* published thus far. One piece of evidence supports this theory. The final plate (unnumbered, F. 536bis) is signed: *Cavalier Piranesi F.* Piranesi was knighted, receiving the title Cavalier, in 1766/67 (the investiture took place in October, 1766; the papal brief was bestowed January 16, 1767). This would seem to indicate that he began the *D'Albano* in 1764, worked on it for a year or two and added the last page only after he was knighted. On the other hand, Hind reports that the Catalogue of 1792 dates the *approbatio* January 5, 1762 (Hind, page 86). If this is correct, then 1764 should be the year of completion. The presence of the titles only in our volume would, in that case, simply be due to conscious choice, or carelessness.

Catalogue Number 40. DI DUE SPELONCHE (Designated Part II of Volume [VIII] of Sackler Set)*

Etched title page:
DI DUE SPELONCHE / ORNATE DAGLI ANTICHI / ALLA RIVA DEL LAGO / ALBANO.

Piranesi here describes two caves on the shore of Lago Albano transformed by the Romans into shrines dedicated to the Nymphs (Nymphaea). One, known today as the *Ninfeo Bergantino*, is located on the west side of the lake, below Castel Gandolfo. Its plan and sculptural decoration is very close to the celebrated Grotto of Tiberius at Sperlonga.

The other is on the north side of the lake towards Marino. It is called the *Ninfeo Dorico* because of its Doric frieze with triglyphs and frieze metopes. These constitute the subject matter of the text and plates I–VIII. Neither discussed in the text nor included in the list of plates are plates IX–XII. These latter depict the terrace and underground corridor (cryptoporticus) of the Villa of Domitian at Castel Gandolfo called by Piranesi the Villa of Clodius. They are situated on the grounds of the papal summer residence, in Piranesi's time the Villa Barberini.

*The volume has been opened to the title page of *Antichità di Cora*. Therefore, this page will not be seen.

This brief work, dating 1762–64, has no proper title page and seems to have been planned as an appendix to the *Emissario del Lago Albano*. In the first sentence of the text, Piranesi speaks of the latter as having been "ultimamente dati all luce," i.e., lately published.

COLLATION: Letterpress p. [1–10]. Twelve etched plates numbered I–XII. Plates II, IV–VII are double. Plate VIII is double folded (two double plates pasted together and folded three times). One etched illustration in the text.

CONTENTS: P. [1] Letterpress caption title (quoted above); p. [1–10] (A–B3): [1] – 5, DI DUE SPELONCHE . . . ; [6]–9, SPIEGAZIONE / DELLE TAVOLE; [10] APPROVAZIONE / . . . / Roma 30. Agosto 1762; vignette on p. [1] (F. 492); plate I–XII (F. 493–504).

WATERMARKS: Hind's type 3.

NOTES: The *Approvazione* (page 10) is dated August 30, 1762.

Catalogue Number 41. ANTICHITÀ DI CORA (Designated Part III of Volume [VIII] of Sackler Set)

Etched title page:
ANTICHITÀ / DI / CORA / DESCRITTE ED INCISE / DA GIOVAMBAT / PIRANESI

Cori (in antiquity — Cora) is an ancient town in southern Lazio, southeast of Rome. Piranesi here describes and illustrates its chief ancient monuments. Plate I shows the remains of the ancient walls built of massive blocks. Plate II is devoted to the Temple of Castor and Pollux, which was rebuilt in the first century B.C. All that remains of it are two Corinthian columns and a section of the architrave. Plate III contains four miscellaneous pieces of decorative stone carving. All the rest of the plates (IIII — X, plus that on the verso of page 15) show the celebrated temple of Hercules. This temple, believed to date from the late second century B.C., has a deep portico (or pronaus) supported by eight slender Doric columns. There are four in the front (tetrastyle) and two on each side.

The external evidence for dating this work 1763–64 has been given in *A Note about the Etchings*.

COLLATION: Letterpress p. [1–2, 1]–15. Etched title page and twelve plates on eleven leaves numbered I–X. An unnumbered etched plate is printed on the verso of page 15. Plates III and [IIIbis] are two small plates on one leaf. Plates II, IIII–VI, VIII and X are double. Plate I is double folded (two double plates pasted together and folded twice). One etched illustration in text.

CONTENTS: P. [1] Half-title; p. [2] blank; etched title page (quoted above) (F. 537); p. [1]-15(A-D2): ANTICHITA DI CORA; vignette on p. [1](F.538); unnumbered plate printed on verso of p. 15 (D2 verso) (F. 539); Plates I–X (F. 540–550).

WATERMARKS: Hind's type 3.

Catalogue Number 42. DELLA MAGNIFICENZA ED ARCHITETTURA DE' ROMANI (Designated Volume [IX] of Sackler Collection at Avery Library)

Etched title page (Latin):
IOANNIS BAPTISTAE / PIRANESII / ANTIQVARIORVM / REGIAE SOCIETATIS LONDINENSIS / SOCII / DE / ROMANORVM / MAGNIFICENTIA / ET ARCHITECTVRA / ROMAE MDCCLXI / Piranesius Archit. Venetus fe

Etched title page (Italian):
DELLA / MAGNIFICENZA / ED ARCHITETTVRA / DE' ROMANI / OPERA / DI GIO BATTISTA PIRANESI / SOCIO DELLA REALE / ACCADEMIA / DEGLI ANTIQVARI / DI LONDRA / Piranesi F

Della magnificenza is Piranesi's manifesto of *Romanità*, his impassioned plea for the recognition of Roman civilization in the face of the ever increasing ascendancy of the Greek faction, led of course by the great and profoundly influential Johann Joachim Winckelmann (1717–1768). It is certain that from the second decade of his career the systematic and scientific exploration of the remains of Rome led Piranesi to an ever increasing interest in artistic theory and the history of civilization. Piranesi's theoretical and polemic writings, though extensive and to himself clearly of the highest importance, are so vastly overshadowed by his *oeuvre* as a graphic artist, that they have not as yet received their due attention. Even Piranesi's friends and contemporaries looked upon his theories with a patronizing and often mocking air and, from the earliest biographers on, doubt has been cast on the authenticity of his critical writings. In recent years a small number of serious studies has thrown new light on limited aspects of Piranesi's thought, but more research, preferably based on a critical edition of the texts, is needed to elucidate his sources and evaluate his place in the mainstream of Enlightenment esthetics.

The publication of *Della magnificenza* in 1761 was the culmination of Piranesi's career as a writer with approximately one hundred pages each of Latin and Italian text on facing pages followed by thirty-eight plates, only a few among them illustrating passages in the text. The role of the plates, one suspects, is to help sell the massive volume, to adorn rather than to illustrate it. If the texts that accompany Piranesi's early volumes are sporadic and mostly introductory, the letterpress grows longer and more important in the succeeding publications of the fifties. The ratio of text to plates changes radically in 1761 with the publication of the *Della magnificenza*.

Though written against the rising tide of the "Grecians," Piranesi's polemic is specifically directed against two works, *The Investigator*, an anonymous pamphlet published in London in 1755, whose author was in fact that same Allan Ramsay who at the very time of its publication had been one of Piranesi's circle of friends — and had earned the special honor of being eternalized on an inscription on one of the monuments of the frontispiece of Volume II of the *Antichità*; and *Les ruines des plus beaux monuments de la Grece*, by D. Le Roy, which had appeared in Paris in 1758 to universal acclaim. Against these two authors, whose general thesis was that Greek architecture is not only superior to Roman, but that in fact without the Greek models Roman architecture would not exist, Piranesi maintained that Roman architecture was based on that of the Etruscans and thus continued the indigenous, Latin tradition. For Piranesi the splendors of Roman functional architecture, such as the aqueducts, the roads or the Cloaca Maxima, the heritage, according to him, of ancient Tusculum, were the true incarnations of Roman magnificence. Against them he disparages Greek architecture, accusing it of overrich ornateness and frivolous caprice. Yet in the face of his own theories, the artist and recorder of Roman antiquities cannot resist the appeal of the luxuriance of Roman ornament.

REFERENCES: *Calvesi* 1967, pp. 6-11; Focillon I, 1918, pp. 74-88, and 1967 pp. 359-362; Giesecke 1911, pp. 20-24; Hind 1922, p. 84; Kaufmann 1955, pp. 105-111; Robison 1971, pp. 192-193, 204; Smith College catalog, 1961; Vogt-Göknil 1958, pp. 59-62; Wittkower 1937/8, pp. 147-158.

Charlotte Rice

COLLATION: Letterpress p. [1–2, i]—CCXXI, two etched title pages, portrait and thirty-eight plates numbered I–XXXVIII. Plates VI, VIII, XI, XIV, XX, XXXV, XXXVII–XXXVIII are double. Plates XVII–XIX and XXX are double folded (for descriptions, see notes). Five etched illustrations in the text (including initials).

CONTENTS: Etched title page, Latin (quoted above) (F. 927); etched title page, Italian (quoted above) (F. 929); Portrait of Pope Clement XIII, signed: Ioannes Baptista Piranesius invenit. Dominicus Cunego, et Piranesius sculpserunt (F. 928); p. [1–2] Dedication: CLEMENTI XIII. / PONT. OPT. MAX.; initial on p. [1] (F. 930); p. [i]–CCXII (a–ggg2): [1] APPROBATIO / . . . / 27. Maii 1760; p. ii–cxcix, Latin text (DE / ROMANORUM / MAGNIFICENTIA / ET ARCHITECTURA) on the even numbered pages facing the Italian version of the text (DELLA / MAGNIFICENZA / ED ARCHITETTURA / DE' ROMANI) on the odd numbered pages; p. [cc] blank; p. cci–ccvi, INDEX / RERUM NOTABILIUM; p. ccvii–CCXII, INDICE / DELLE COSE NOTABILI; initial "D" with Capitoline wolf on p. ii, unsigned, 82 x 100 mm. [NOT LISTED BY FOCILLON]; initial on p. iii (F. 931); tail-piece on p. cxcviii which depicts two reliefs each showing the temple of Jupiter on the Capitoline; the caption begins: *AB Frons, sive pronaum templi Iovis Capitolini* . . . ; signed, lower right: Piranesi F.; 192 x 291 mm. [NOT LISTED BY FOCILLON]; tail-piece on p. cxcix (F. 932) — F. cites p. XXXVI; plates I–XXXVIII (F. 933–966). Focillon did not list Plates XVII–XIX and XXX, but these are described below in the notes.

WATERMARKS: Hind's type 3.

DIMENSIONS OF VOLUME: H. 22⅝" (575 mm.) W. 16¾" (425 mm.)

IMPRESSIONS: Most of the plates are printed in black ink, a few verging toward brown or sepia.

BINDING AND CONDITION: Bound in full contemporary vellum. On spine, six panels with gilt ornaments and a seventh (second from the top) with the following title: PIRANESI / DE ROMANO. / MAGNIFICE. / ET ARCHIT. Top and bottom panels partly missing. Vellum split along front hinge and at the top of back hinge. Fore-edges sprinkled. Blank flyleaves.

NOTES: On the recto of the front flyleaf, a printed label: *Arbury Library*. The *Approbatio* is dated May 27, 1760. Focillon fails to list two illustrations, an initial and a tail-piece, in the Latin text. These have been described above in the contents. He seems to have based his list on a copy with the Italian text only. The following plates are also missing from Focillon:

XVII. Twenty-four architectural fragments, including thirteen capitals, each with a caption giving its location. To right of center, a frieze and architrave fragment inscribed *In Hortis Palatinis Farnesianis*. Signed lower left: Piranesi F. Two double plates pasted together and folded five times (ca. 417 x ca. 1226 mm.)

XVIII. Seventeen architectural fragments, plus cross sections of three of them, each with a caption giving its location. To left of center, a cornice fragment: *Transtiberim prope Pontem Senatorium* . . . Signed lower right: Piranesi F. Two double plates pasted together and folded five times (ca. 415 x ca. 1220 mm.)

XIX. Twenty-five architectural fragments, each identified with a caption, letter or number. To right of center, a massive entablature: *Supra valvas templi SS. Cosmae et Damiani*. Signed lower right: Piranesi F. Two double plates pasted together and folded five times (ca. 413 x ca. 1230 mm.).

XXX. *Schemata Emissarii Lacus Albani*. Three representations, the second and third depicted as pinned onto the main one. Fig. I, *Sectio scenographia epistomii* . . . Fig. II. *Scenographia frontis* . . . Fig. III. *Scenographia ruderum castelli, quo aqua lacus Albani* . . . Signed lower left: Piranesi F. Two double plates folded together and folded five times (ca. 402 x ca. 1123 mm.).

Bound in the same volume with the *Della magnificenza* is a supplement entitled *Osservazioni di Gio. Battista Piranesi sopra la Lettre de M. Mariette* . . . (1765), described in *Catalogue Number 43*.

Catalogue Number 43. OSSERVAZIONI.*

Etched title page:
Osservazioni / Di Gio. Battista Piranesi / sopra la / Lettre de M. Mariette aux Auteur de la Gazette / Littèraire de l'Europe, / Inserita nel / Supplemento dell' istessa / Gazzetta stampata / Dimanche 4. Novembre / MDCCLIV. / E Parere su l'Architettura, con una Prefazione ad un nuo/vo Trattato della introduzione e del progresso delle / belle arti in Europa ne' tempi antichi. / In Roma / M.DCC.LXV. / Con licenza / de' Superiori. / Piranesi F.

A critique of Piranesi's work from the Grecian faction appeared in the *Gazette Litteraire de l'Europe* in 1764 — four years after the publication of *Della magnificenza ed architettura de romani*. The author was the French collector and connoisseur J. P. Mariette. Stung into a reply and anxious to publish it without further delay, Piranesi seems to have had difficulties assembling enough material for even a slender volume. The volume is divided into three parts. Only the first eight pages, including a reprint of Mariette's letter, carry on Piranesi's polemic with the Frenchman. The second part of the volume, the *Parere su l'architettura*, is a dialogue concerning architectural matters. The third and last part represents what was to be the introductory chapter of a projected but never realized history of ancient art. By far the most important and original part of the book is the *Parere*; even as a dialogue, a literary form much favored at the time, the *Parere* can hold its own. Its greatest interest, however, lies in the theme, which is the vindication of the architect as an original and creative artist. On the face of it Piranesi seems to have had a serious change of heart since writing *Della magnificenza*, where he had attacked ornament in architecture, for now he not only praises it but also considers it as quintessential. The explanation is that in the earlier work Piranese spoke as an archaeologist, in favor of Rome.

In the *Parere* we hear the voice of the practicing architect, deeply involved with two projects, the remodelling of San

*Not exhibited.

Giovanni in Laterano and that of Santa Maria del Priorato. Where previously he invoked order, simplicity and the absolute rule of Vitruvius and Palladio, he now claims, having become a creative architect himself, autonomy for the artist and the right to give his exuberant imagination free play.

An issue of some importance for the dating of the last six plates of the *Osservazioni* volume and, by extension, for the dating of a number of other works which have been traditionally ascribed to the middle 1760's, is raised by the fact that from plate IV on, Piranesi uses for his signature the newly acquired title of *Cavaliere del Sperone d'Oro*, a papal order or chivalry given to distinguished artists of that time.

The title page of the *Osservazioni* volume is dated 1765. It was, however, only after January 16, 1767, the date of the papal brief bestowing the order of the Golden Spur upon Piranesi, that he was able to use the new title. Although Clement XIII Rezzonico had long been a patron of his fellow Venetian, it was in connection with Piranesi's sole executed architectural commission, the restoration and refurbishing of Santa Maria del Priorato, under the patronage of Cardinal Gianbattista Rezzonico, nephew of the Pope, and Prior of the Knights of Malta, that the Pope knighted Piranesi. Legrand, Piranesi's earliest French biographer, tells us that the investiture was held in the church when the Pope came to view it on its completion. There is a detailed account of this ceremony, which took place on the second Monday of October 1766, in the October 15 issue of the weekly journal *Diario di Roma* of that year.

It is of course possible that the word *cavaliere* was a subsequent addition to the signature on plates IV to IX of the *Osservazioni*; a number of convincing arguments makes this unlikely: First of all, there are no known impressions of plates IV to IX without the new title in the signature. Second, if Piranesi had decided to add the new title to the signature several years later, he would surely have done so on all the plates. Third, copies of the *Osservazioni* volumes apparently fall into three groups: 1. the text followed by plates I to III only; 2. the text followed by numbered plates I to III and the six remaining plates unnumbered; 3. the text followed by the complete set of nine numbered plates. These discrepancies in the makeup of the volume point to the likelihood that plates IV to IX are later additions, etched or at any rate published after Piranesi received his knighthood. Finally, in the last paragraph of the *Parere*, Piranesi himself tells us that he is preparing, in addition to his history of ancient art, the publication of the drawings that had been the subject of discussion on the preceding pages.

REFERENCES: Focillon 1963, pp. 362–363; Giesecke 1912, p. 31; Diario di Roma 1766, (#7695), pp. 5–13; Harris 1967, pp. 189–196; Kaufmann 1955, pp. 107–108; Legrand 1922, pp. 62–63; Robison 1971, p. 193; Smith Catalogue, 1961; Turin Catalogue, 1961, #194, ill. 119 and #195, ill. 120; Stillman 1967, pp. 199–201; Vogt-Göknil 1958, pp. 63–69; Wittkower 1938/9, pp. 150–158.

COLLATION: Letterpress p. [1]-16[17]18-23. Etched title page and ten plates of which three are numbered I–III. An unnumbered plate is printed on the verso of p. 23. There are also six unnumbered double plates. Five etched illustrations in text.

CONTENTS: Etched title page (quoted above) (F. 967); p. [1]-16 (A-D2): [1]-8 OSSERVAZIONI / DI GIO. BATTISTA PIRANESI / SOPRA LA / Lettre de Monsieur Mariette . . . ; [9]–16, PARERE / SU L'ARCHITET-TURA; vignette on p. [1] (F. 968); vignette on p. [9] (F. 969); tail-piece on p. 16 (F. 970); Plates [IV, VI, V, VII, VIII, IX] (F. 977, 979, 978, 980–982); p. [17]–23 (E–[F2]): DELLA INTRODUZIONE / E DEL PROGRESSO DELLE BELLE ARTI / IN EUROPA / NE TEMPI ANTICHI; vignette on p. [17] (F. 971); tail-piece on p. 23 (F. 972); unnumbered plate printed on verso on p. 23 (F. 973); plates I–III (F. 974–976).

WATERMARKS: Hind's type 3.

NOTES: This work is normally bound as a supplement to *Della magnificenza* . . . The six unnumbered plates (F. 977, 979, 978, 980–982) were later numbered IV–IX and bound after Plates I–III (F. 974–976).

Charlotte Rice

Abbreviations and Symbols*

Colnaghi | Colnaghi (P & D) & Company, Ltd., London.
Etchings by Giovanni Battista Piranesi.

F. | Focillon, Henri
   Giovanni-Battista Piranesi, essai de catalogue raissone de son oeuvre...
   The basic list of Piranesi's plates, though not quite complete.

Hind | Hind, Arthur Mayger
   Giovanni Battista Piranesi, A Critical Study.
   The first, still essential, attempt to distinguish the different states of the *Carceri* and the *Vedute di Roma* and with a list of Piranesi's published works.

Robison I | Robison, Andrew
   "Giovanni Battista Piranesi: Prolegomena to the Princeton collections."

Robison II | Robison, Andrew
   "The 'Vedute di Roma' of Giovanni Battista Piranesi; notes towards a revision of Hind's catalogue."

[] | Numbers which have been assigned for identification purposes but which do not appear on original plate are given square brackets.

/ | Indicates where a line in the original text ends.

. . . | Title has not been fully quoted.

*See Bibliography for the full citation of books and periodicals referred to here.

Selective Bibliography

Adhemar, Jean et Mme. Bonefant. *Piranèse*, [Exposition] Galerie Mansart, Bibliothèque Nationale, Paris, 1962.

Associazione Francesco Francia. *Mostra di incisioni di G. B. Piranesi*, [Exhibition] Bologna, 1963.

Bacou, Rosaline. *Piranèse, Gravures et dessins*, Paris, 1975.

_____ . *Piranesi* (English translation), Boston, 1975.

Bean, Jacob and Stampfle, Felice. *The Eighteenth Century in Italy*, Drawings from New York Collections, III, [Exhibition at the Metropolitan Museum of Art] New York, 1971.

Biagi, Pietro. *Sull'incisione e sul Piranesi*, Venice, 1820.

Bianconi, G. L. "Elogio storico del Cav. G. B. Piranesi," *Antologia Romana*, 1779, nos. 34, 35 and 36 and G. L. Bianconi, *Opere*, 1802, ii, pp. 127–140.

British Museum. *Giovanni Battista Piranesi: His Predecessors and His Heritage*, [Exhibition] London, 1968.

Calcographie des Piranesi frères. *Œuvres de Jean-Baptiste et de Francois qui se vendent chez les Auteurs*, a Paris rue l'Universitè, Depot des Machines, no. 296, pp. 18, Paris, 1800.

Christie, Manson and Woods. *Fine Old Master Drawings, March 30, 1971*, London, 1971.

Colnaghi (P & D) & Company, Ltd. *Etchings by Giovanni Battista Piranesi, 1720–1778*, [Exhibition, December 1973–January 1974] London, 1973.

Columbia University, Avery Architectural Library. *Giovanni Battista Piranesi Drawings and Etchings at Columbia University*, [Exhibition at Low Memorial Library, March 21 – April 14, 1972] New York, 1972.

Craig, Maurice James. *The Volunteer Earl, being the life and times of James Caulfield, first earl of Charlemont*, London, The Cresset Press, 1948.

Diario di Roma. n. 7695, dated 25 October 1766, pp. 5–13.

Fasolo, Vincenzo. "Il Campomarzio di G. B. Piranesi" *Quaderni dell' Istituto di Storia dell' Architettura*, XV (1956) pp. 1–14.

Fischer, Manfred F. "Die Umbaupläne des Giovanni Battista Piranesi für den Chor in S. Giovanni in Laterno," *Münchner Jahrbuch der bildenden Kunst*, 1968 (XIX) pp. 207–228.

Fleming, John. *Robert Adam and his Circle in Edinburgh and Rome*, London, 1962.

Focillon, Henri. *Giovanni-Battista Piranesi 1720–1778*, Paris, 1918.

_____ . *Giovanni Battista Piranesi*, Nouvelle edition, Paris, 1963.

_____ . *Giovanni-Battista Piranesi, essai de catalogue raisonne de son oeuvre*, Paris, 1918.

_____ . *Giovanni Battista Piranesi*, eds. M. Calvesi and A. Monferini, Bologna, 1967.

Giesecke, Albert. *Giovanni Battista Piranesi*, Leipzig, 1911.

Harris, John. "Le Geay, Piranesi and International Neoclassicism in Rome 1740–1750," *Essays in the History of Architecture Presented to Rudolf Wittkower*, London, 1967, pp. 189–196.

Hermanin, Federico. *Giambattista Piranesi*, Rome, 1922. [cover 1923]

Hind, Arthur M. *Giovanni Battista Piranesi, A Critical Study*, London, 1922.

_____ . *Giovanni Battista Piranesi, A Critical Study*, New York, 1967.

Honour, Hugh. *Neo-classicism*, Baltimore, 1968.

Huxley, Aldous Leonard. *Prisons* (with the "Carceri" etchings), London, 1940.

Kaufmann, Emil. *Architecture in the Age of Reason*, Cambridge, Mass., 1955.

Keller, Luzius. *Piranèse et les Romantiques francais*, Paris, 1966.

Kennedy, James (probable author). *Life of the Chevalier Giovanni Battista Piranesi*, The Library of Fine Arts, London, Vol. II, August, 1831, pp. 8–13.

Korte, Werner. "Giovanni Battista Piranesi als praktischer Architekt," *Zeitschrift für Kunstgeschichte*, neue Folge, Vol. II, 1933, pp. 16–33.

Legrand, J. G. *Notice historique sur la vie et les oeuvres de G. B. Piranesi*, Manuscript 5968 in the Bibliothèque Nationale, Paris, printed in G. Morazzoni, *Giovan Battista Piranesi, Architetto ed Incisore (1720–1778)* cited below in the bibliography; and [Bibliothèque Nationale, Cabinet des estampes] *Nouvelles de l'estampe* no. 5, 1969.

Madrid, Biblioteca nacional. *Giovanni Battista Piranesi en la Biblioteca nacional. Estudio preliminar y catalogo por Enrique Lafuente Ferrari*. Madrid, 1936.

Mariani, Valerio. . . . *Studiando Piranesi*, Rome, 1938.

Mayor, A. Hyatt. *Giovanni Battista Piranesi*, New York, 1952.

Meeks, Carroll L. V. *Italian Architecture 1750–1914*, New Haven, 1966.

Morazzoni, G. *Giovan Battista Piranesi, Architetto ed Incisore (1720–1778)*, Rome, 1921.

Munoz, Antonio. *G. B. Piranesi*, Rome, 1920.

Murray, Peter. *Piranesi and the grandeur of ancient Rome*, London, 1971.

Piranesi, Francesco and Pietro. *Oeuvres des Chevaliers Jean-Baptiste et Francois Piranesi qu'on vend separement dans la Calcographie des auteurs, Rue Felice, pres de la Trinité des Monts, & c.* pp. 29. Rome 1792.

Piranesi, Giovanni Battista. *Giambattista Piranesi, architetto ed incisore. Cinquanta tavole con introduzione di Federico Hermanin*, Torino, 1915.

Piranesi, Giovanni Battista. *Magnificenza di Roma*. Con una introduzione di Mario Praz e note illustrative di Livio Jannattoni, Milano, 1961.

Piranesi, Giovanni Battista. *The Prisons (Le Carceri); the complete first and second states*. With a new introduction by Philip Hofer. New York, 1973.

Prague, Narodni Galerie. *Giovanni Battista Piranesi, 1720–1778; grafické dílo.* [Exhibition] 1972.

Robison, Andrew. "Giovanni Battista Piranesi: Prolegomena to the Princeton collections," *The Princeton University Library Chronicle*, XXXI, 1970, pp. 165–206.

_____ . "The 'Vedute di Roma' of Giovanni Battista Piranesi," [Bibliothèque Nationale, Cabinet des estampes]. Nouvelles de l'estampe, no. 4, 1970, leaves 180–198.

Rohault de Fleury, George. *Le Latran au moyen age*, Paris, 1877.

Rome, Calcografia nazionale. *Catalogo generale delle stampe tratte dai rami incisi posseduti dalla Calcografia nazionale di Carlo Alberto Petrucci*, Rome, 1953.

_____ . Calcografia nazionale. *Giovanni Battista e Francesco Piranesi*, [Exhibition] Rome, 1967-68.

Samuel, Arthur. *Piranesi*. London, 1910.

Smith College Museum of Art. *Piranesi* [Exhibition] Northampton, Mass., 1961.

Stampfle, Felice. "An Unknown Group of Drawings by Giovanni Battista Piranesi," *Art Bulletin*, XXX, 1948, pp. 122–141.

_____ . *Giovanni Battista Piranesi, An Exhibition of Drawings* [The Pierpont Morgan Library, New York, 1949.]

Stillman, Damie. "Robert Adam and Piranesi," *Essays in the History of Architecture Presented to Rudolf Wittkower*, London, 1967, pp. 197–206.

Sturgis, Russell. *The Etchings of Piranesi*. New York, 1905.

Thomas, Hylton. *The Drawings of Giovanni Battista Piranesi*, London, 1954.

Turin, Museo Civico. *G. B. Piranesi, acqueforti e disegni.* [Exhibition dicembre 1961 — gennaio 1962] Torino, 1961.

Vogt-Göknil, Ulya. *Giovanni Battista Piranesi, Carceri*, Zurich, 1958.

Volkmann, Hans. *Giovanni Battista Piranesi, Architekt und Graphiker*, Berlin, 1965.

Watson, Francis J. B. "A Side Table by Piranesi, A Masterpiece of Neo-Classic Furniture," *The Minneapolis Institute of Arts Bulletin*, LIV, 1965, pp. 19–29.

Wiebenson, Dora. *Sources of Greek Revival Architecture*, London, 1969.

Wilton-Ely, John, ed. *Giovanni Battista Piranesi, the Polemical Works, Rome 1757, 1761, 1765, 1769*, Farnborough, Hants., England, 1972.

Wittkower, Rudolf. *Art and Architecture in Italy 1600–1750*, 3rd ed., Baltimore, Md., 1973.

_____ . "Piranesi as Architect," *Piranesi* [Exhibition, Smith College Museum of Art], Northampton, Mass., 1961.

_____ . "Piranesi's *Parere su l'architettura*," *Journal of the Warburg Institute*, II, 1938-9, pp. 147–158.